Franchere's Journal

A Voyage to the Northwest Coast of America

The Founding of Astoria

Franchere's Journal

A Voyage to the Northwest Coast of America

The Founding of Astoria

By Gabriel Franchere

Editor

J.L. Smith, M.A.

White Stone Press

Anchorage, Alaska

2014

ISBN 13: 978-1501075575

ISBN 10: 1501075578

Printed in the United States of America

The cover painted by Emily Schultz

To Hannah

Contents

Franchere's[1] Journal

A Voyage to the Northwest Coast of America

Chapter One
Weighing Anchor in Hawaii

Having taken on board a hundred head of live hogs, some goats, two sheep, a quantity of poul-

---

[1] FRANCHERE, Gabriel, explorer, born in Montreal, 3 November 1786; died in St. Paul, Minnesota, in 1856. He was educated in Montreal, and trained to commercial pursuits by his father. In 1810 he bound himself for five years to the Pacific fur company, formed by John Jacob Astor, and was a member of the expedition sent to develop the fur trade beyond the Rocky Mountains. He returned to New York with several of his companions in less than two months, and in September 1810, sailed on the *Tonquin* for the Columbia River, where the expedition arrived in March 1811, after suffering many hardships. Franchere was one of the witnesses to the transfer of Astoria to the Northwest company, after the breaking out of hostilities between the United States and England, and remained for some time in the service of that company, but finally resolved to return to Canada. In order to reach Montreal he traveled a distance of 5,000 miles by the overland route in canoes or on foot. Franchere removed to Sault Ste. Marie in 1834, and engaged in the fur trade. He afterward established the commercial house of Franchere and Company in New York City. He was the last survivor of the Astor expedition. (*www.3rd1000.com/history*)

try, two boat-loads of sugar cane to feed the hogs, as many more of yams, taro, and other vegetables, and all our water-casks being snugly stowed, we weighed anchor on the 28th of February, sixteen days after our arrival at Karakakoua.

We left another man (Edward Aymes)[2] at Wahoo. He belonged to a boat's crew which was

---

[2] Seventeen year old Edward Aymes joined John Astor's *Tonquin* as a seaman before September 3, 1810 and sailed five days later from New York Harbor. In February 1811, after reaching the Hawaiian Islands, he tried to desert but was caught, tied up and flogged. Eventually he was left at Oahu, an act the paradoxically saved his life. He was sent ashore for a load of sugarcane that he and others loaded on a boat that had been left high and dry by the ebb tide. Believing that he had considerable time, he took a stroll but, during his absence, the tide came in and the captain's younger brother, James C. Thorn, left without him. Aymes had to hire a canoe that took him to the side of the *Tonquin*, whereupon the captain got into the boat and beat Aymes unmercifully, throwing him overboard. Aymes clothes were then thrown into the canoe and the *Tonquin* sailed without him. Brutal as the incident was, it saved Aymes from the fate of his fellow crew members. He appears to have stayed in the islands until October 7, 1811 when he shipped onto the Salem brig *New Hazard* along with fellow seamen Joseph Wings, Samuel Pace and Immanuel Pinto, but didn't do well on this voyage either. On October 29, 1811, on his way back of the coast, Aymes let go of the brace block twice and consequently was flogged by the 2nd mate with a "piece of ratline stuff." His relations with the 2nd mate remained tenuous for the next year, and on September 20, 1812 while enroute to the Hawaiian Islands, Gale accused Aymes of stealing the fore hatch key, later located in the armor's forge,

sent ashore for a load of sugar canes. By the time the boat was loaded by the natives the ebb of the tide had left her aground, and Aymes asked leave of the coxswain to take a stroll, engaging to be back for the flood. Leave was granted him, but during his absence, the tide having come in sufficiently to float the boat, James Thorn, the coxswain, did not wait for the young sailor, who was thus left behind. The captain immediately missed the man, and on being informed that he had strolled away from the boat on leave, flew into a violent passion. Aymes soon made his appearance alongside, having hired some natives to take him on board; on perceiving him, the captain[3] ordered him to stay in the

---

and flogged him. For his supposed crime, he was sent "to the main-top cross" till twelve o'clock in the morning. A few weeks later, on October 18, 1812, he went ashore at Honolulu harbor and disappeared from records. He likely joined another vessel. (BC Mdtis) .

[3] Jonathan Thorn was a sixth-generation descendant of William Thorne, who arrived in Massachusetts from England in 1638. Jonathon entered the United States Navy on 28 April 1800 as a midshipman and was promoted acting lieutenant on 7 Nov. 1803. He served with distinction the Barbary Wars, in February 1804 participating in Stephen Decatur's celebrated raid into the harbor of Tripoli (Libya) to destroy the grounded American frigate *Philadelphia* . On June 6, 1805, at the early age of 26, Thorne was appointed commandant of the New York Navy Yard

longboat, then lashed to the side with its load of sugar cane. The captain then himself got into the boat, and, taking one of the canes, beat the poor fellow most unmercifully with it; after which, not satisfied with this act of brutality, he seized his victim and threw him overboard! Aymes, however, being an excellent swimmer, made for the nearest native canoe, of which there were, as usual, a great number around the ship. The Islanders, more humane than our captain, took in the poor fellow, who, in spite of his entreaties to be received on board, could only succeed in getting his clothes which were thrown into the canoe. At parting, he told Captain Thorn that he knew enough of the laws of his country, to obtain redress, should they ever meet in the territory of the American Union.

While we were getting under sail, Mr. McKay pointed out to the captain that there was one water-cask empty, and proposed sending it ashore to be filled, as the great number of live ani-

and on 16 Feb. 1807 received his lieutenancy. On 18 May 1810, at the request of John Astor, he was granted a two-year furlough. Astor had purchased half interest in the 269 ton *Tonquin* in August of that year from the German builder. She sailed from New York on 6 September 1810.

mals we had on board required a large quantity of fresh water. The captain, who feared that some of the men would desert if he sent them a-shore, made an observation to that effect in answer to Mr. McKay[4], who then proposed sending me in a canoe which lay alongside to fill the cask in question: this was agreed to by the Captain, and I took the cask accordingly to the nearest spring. Having filled it, not without some difficulty, the Islanders seeking to detain me and I perceiving that they had given me some gourds full of salt water, I was forced also to demand a double pirogue (for the canoe which had brought the empty cask, was found inadequate to carry a full one) the ship being already under full sail and gaining an offing. As the natives would not lend

---

[4] The *Tonquin* replenished its supply of fresh water at the bleak Falkland Islands, off the coast of South America. Five of McKay's business associates were a few minutes late getting back to the beach; so Thorn lifted anchor without them. The five, sure they were to be left behind to perish as castaways, rowed frantically after *the Tonquin* for three hours. It was reported that Robert Strauss had place a pistol to Thorn's head and told he that if he didn't stop for the five passengers, Strauss would blow is brains out. Later Thorn wrote Astor that only the opportune waning of the wind, which left the *Tonquin* becalmed, enabled the five wretched men to overtake the bark. This experience terrified all on board.

a hand to procure what I wanted, I thought it necessary to have recourse to the King,[5] and in fact did so. For seeing the vessel so far at sea, with what I knew of the captain's disposition, I began to fear that he had formed the plan of leaving me on the Island. My fears, nevertheless, were ill-founded; the vessel made a tack toward the shore, to my great joy; and a double pirogue was furnished me, through the good offices of our young friend, the French school-master, to return on board with my cask.

---

[5] Tamehameha, king of all the Sandwich Islands. The remarkable Tamehameha I was occasionally called the "Napoleon of the Pacific." Before his reign, the Islands were in a semi-feudal state, each with its own chief and lesser vassals. Tamehameha (born in 1736), was chieftain of a portion of Hawaii, and after the death of Kalaniopuu (called Tereoboo by Cook) took advantage of a disputed succession, and by means of a sanguinary war of nearly nine years (1782-91) made himself master of the entire Island. Aided by European arms and advice, he gradually subjugated the neighboring islands; the great battle of Nuuanu Valley in 1795 putting him in final possession of Oahu (Wahoo). Later (1803), the lord of Kauai (Atouay) submitted to Tamehameha, who thus became absolute king over the entire island group. He remained at Oahu until 1813, when he returned to his native Hawaii, where he died in May, 1819. Tamehameha was a man of great force of character, and his reign was the beginning of law and order in the Hawaiian archipelago. He appointed subordinate governors on each island, instituted a regular system of taxation or tribute, made some progress in enforcing justice, and ruled in the way of a benevolent despot. (Early Western Travels...)

Our deck was now as much encumbered as when we left New York; for we had been obliged to place our live animals at the gangways, and to board over their pens, on which it was necessary to pass, to work on the ship. Our own numbers were also augmented; for we had taken a dozen Islanders for the service of our intended commercial establishment. Their term of engagement was three years, during which time we were to feed and clothe them, and at its expiration they were to receive a hundred dollars in merchandise. The captain had shipped another dozen as hands on the coasting voyage. These people, who make very good sailors, were eager to be taken into employment and we might easily have carried off a much greater number.

We had contrary winds till the 2d of March, when, having doubled the western extremity of the island, we made northing and lost sight of these smiling and temperate countries, to enter very soon a colder region and less worthy of being inhabited. The winds were variable and nothing extraordinary happened to us till the 10th, when, being arrived at the latitude of 35° 11' north, and in 138° 16' of west longitude, the wind shifted all of a sudden to the S.S.W., and blew with such violence, that we were forced to strike top-gallant masts and top-sails, and run before the gale with a double reef in our foresail.[6] The rolling of the vessel was greater than in all the gales we had experienced previously. Nevertheless, as we made great headway, and were approaching the continent, the captain by way of precaution lay to for two nights successively. At last, on the 22d, in the morning, we saw the land. Although we had not been able to take any observations for several days, nevertheless, by the appearance of the coast, we perceived that we were near the mouth of the river Columbia, and were not more than three miles from land. The breakers formed by the bar at the entrance of that river, and which we could distinguish

---

[6] Ross notes: During this storm, almost everything on deck was carried off or dashed to pieces; all of our livestock were either killed or washed overboard. The Headquarters log listed the following animals landed: 1 ewe and 1 ram, 8 goats, viz. 3 males and 1 female, 14 hogs, to wit, 4 males and 10 females, two which, 1 male and 1 female made their escape into the woods before they could be got into the pen, left 3 hands to attend to them. Thorn took about half of these animal with him when he sailed north a few months later in search of furs.

from the ship, left us no room to doubt that we had arrived at last at the end of our voyage.

The wind was blowing in heavy squalls, and the sea ran very high: in spite of that, the Captain caused a boat to be lowered, and Mr. Fox,[7] Basile Lapensee, Ignace Lapensee,[8] Jos. Nadeau[9], and John Martin,[10] got into her, taking some provisions and firearms, with orders to sound the channel and report themselves on board as soon as possible. The boat was not even supplied with a good sail or a mast, but one of the   partners gave   Mr. Fox a pair of bed sheets to serve for the former. Messrs McKay[11] and McDougal[12] could not help remonstrating with the captain on the imprudence of sending the boat ashore in such weather; but they could not move his obstinacy. The boat's crew pulled away from the ship; alas! we were never to see her again; and we already had a foreboding of

---

[7] Ebenezer Fox was first mate on the *Tonquin.* He had previously been to the Northwest.

[8] Basile and Ignace Lapensee were carters from Montreal.

[9] Nadeau was a barber from Montreal.

[10] Martin was a sailor.

[11] Alexander McKay killed in the *Tonquin* incident in late 1811.

[12] Duncan McDougall, later became the head man of North West Co. in Astoria.

her fate.[13] The next day the wind seemed to moderate, and we approached very near the coast. The entrance of the river, which we plainly distinguished with the naked eye, appeared but a confused and agitated sea: the waves, impelled by a wind from the offing, broke upon the bar and left no perceptible passage. We got no sign of the boat; and toward evening for our own safety, we hauled off to sea, with all countenances extremely sad, not excepting the captain's, who appeared to me as much afflicted as the rest, and who had reason to be so. During the night, the wind fell, the clouds dispersed, and the sky

---

[13] Ross records an earlier incident aboard the *Tonquin* that almost resulted in the death of one of the persons on board: On the 11th of February, while sailing on the high seas, a man named Joe Lapierre fell from the main mast-head overboard, the ship was going eight knots - a boat was instantly lowered: in the mean time a hen-coop, binnacle and some boards were thrown into the water, but he failed to get a hold of anything, and soon fell a mile or more astern. When we picked him up he was in a state of insensibility, and the crew made all possible haste to reach the man, but, as they were approaching, the captain, in a peremptory tone, ordered them back to pick up the hen-coop, binnacle, and boards, before they came alone side or put the man on board. The boat obeyed orders, went back again, picked up all, and returned to the ship after 52 minutes - yet the life was not quite extinct, for, after applying the usual remedies of salt, warm blankets, and friction, Lapierre revived. (Early Western Travels...)

became serene. On the morning of the 24th we found that the current had carried us near the coast again, and we dropped anchor in fourteen fathoms water, north of Cape Disappointment. The *coup d'oeil* is not so smiling by a great deal at this anchorage as at the Sandwich Islands, the coast offering little to the eye but a continuous range of high mountains covered with snow.

Although it was calm the sea continued to break over the reef with violence between Cape Disappointment[14] and Point Adams. We sent Mr. Mumford[15] (second mate) to sound a passage;

---

[14] So named by John Meares on the *Felice Adventurer* in 1788. The name of the Cape reflects Meares' disappointment that he was not able to find the mouth of the Columbia River as depicted on the Spanish map in his possession.

[15] When the thirty-three year old Rhode Island native joined the Astor ship *Tonquin* around September 3, 1810, it wasn't the first time he had sailed to the Pacific. Consequently, after a tempestuous voyage around the Horn, when the vessel stopped at the Sandwich Islands, he was able to identify various landmarks. On March 23, 1811 as the *Tonquin* was trying to negotiate its way across the bar of the Columbia River, the apparently short tempered second mate took soundings in what was perhaps unfamiliar territory. This temper, however, saved him for after he had an argument with Thorn, he agreed to stay ashore to take command of the tender *Dolly* thus inadvertently avoiding the fate of his shipmates up the coast. While on shore, however, he would not take orders from Astor's partner Robert Stuart, and so, after a trip up river in the *Dolly* to obtain food, Mumford arrived back alone in a canoe at Fort Astoria on October 17. Sometime after the Astor ship *Beaver* (Cornelius Soule) arrived at Astoria on May 9, 1812, Mumford signed on probably

11

but having found the breakers too heavy, he returned on board about midday. Messrs. McKay and D. Stuart offered their services to go ashore to search for the boat's crew who left on the 22d; but they could not find a place to land. They saw Indians who made signs to them to pull round the Cape, but they deemed it more prudent to return to the vessel. Soon after their return a gentle breeze sprang up from the westward, we raised anchor, and approached the entrance of the river. Mr. Aikin[16] was then dispatched in the pinnace, accompanied by John Coles (sail-maker), Stephen Weeks (armorer) and two Sandwich-islanders and we followed under easy sail. Another boat had been sent out before this one, but the captain judging that she bore too far south, made her a signal to return. Mr. Aikin not finding less than four fathoms, we followed him and advanced between the breakers with a favorable wind, so that we passed the boat

---

as second mate and in August, sailed for Sitka. As the War of 1812 was raging, and fearing capture, the *Beaver* sailed directly to Canton where Capt. Soule had her interned for the rest of the war. Mumford likely returned to New York from Canton on the ship *Beaver*. (BC Metis Mapping Research Project)

[16] Third mate on the *Tonquin*, Aikin was sent to take charge of the tender *Dolly*.

on our starboard, within pistol-shot. We made signs to her to return on board, but she could not accomplish it; the ebb tide carried her with such rapidity that in a few minutes we had lost sight of her amidst the tremendous breakers that surrounded us. It was near nightfall, the wind began to give way, and the water was so low with the ebb that we struck six or seven times with violence: the breakers broke over the ship and threatened to submerge her. At last we passed from two and three-quarters fathoms of water to seven, where we were obliged to drop anchor, the wind having entirely failed us. We were far, however, from being out of danger, and the darkness came to add to the horror of our situation: our vessel, though at anchor, threatened to be carried away every moment by the tide; the best bower was let go and it kept two men at the wheel to hold her head in the right direction. However, Providence came to our succor: the flood succeeded to the ebb, and the wind rising out of the offing, we weighed both anchors, in spite of the obscurity of the night and succeeded in gaining a little bay or cove, formed at the entrance of the river by *Cape Disappointment* and called *Baker's*

Bay,[17] where we found a good anchorage. It was about midnight, and all retired to take a little rest: the crew, above all, had great need of it. We were fortunate to be in a place of safety for the wind rose higher and higher during the rest of the night and on the morning of the 25th allowed us to see that this ocean is not always pacific.

Some natives visited us this day, bringing with them beaver-skins; but the inquietude caused in our minds by the loss of two boats' crews, for whom we wished to make search, did not permit us to think of traffic. We tried to make the savages comprehend by signs that we had sent a boat ashore three days previous and that we had no news of her; but they seemed not to understand us. The captain, accompanied by some of our gentlemen, landed, and they set themselves to search for our missing people, in the woods,

---

[17] Named by William Broughton of the *Chatham*, in 1792 after Captain Baker of the American Brig *Jenny* which he found anchored there upon his return from his voyage up the Columbia River. He intended to give the impression that the American discoveries were limited to shallow bays near the mouth of the river and that prior exploration should be given to the English. Lewis and Clark called the bay "Haley's" after a favorite trader of the Indians; while Sgt. Gass, of the same expedition, called it "Rogue's Harbor because of the knavery if the neighboring Indians (Early Western Travels...).

and along the shore N.W. of the cape. After a few hours we saw the captain return with Weeks, one of the crew of the last boat sent out. He was stark naked, and after being clothed and receiving some nourishment, gave us an account of his almost miraculous escape from the waves on the preceding night, in nearly the following terms:

"After you had passed our boat," said he, "the breakers caused by the meeting of the wind roll and ebb tide became a great deal heavier than when we entered the river with the flood. The boat, for want of a rudder, became very hard to manage, and we let her drift at the mercy of the tide till, after having escaped several surges, one struck us mid ship and capsized us. I lost sight of Mr. Aikin and John Coles[18]: but the two Is-

---

[18] John Coles appears to have replaced sail maker Aaron Slaight on John Astor's *Tonquin* at the last minute as there is no mention of John Coles in the Port of New York ship's manifest of September 3, 1810. This was his tragic mistake. On September 8, 1810, Coles sailed on the *Tonquin* beginning a miserable voyage the Horn. The *Tonquin* arrived the following February at the Hawaiian Islands and on March 22 found itself at the dangerous mouth of the Columbia River. That day, in an attempt to sound the bar for safe passage, a longboat carried five men to their deaths. Two days later, on March 24, still unable to negotiate the bar, the captain ordered John Coles, Job Aikin, Stephen weeks, and Peter and Harry, two Sandwich Islanders, in a small pinnace to take soundings while the *Tonquin* followed under easy sail. However,

landers were close by me; I saw the stripping off their clothes, and I followed their example; and seeing the pinnace within my reach, keel upward, I seized it; the two natives came to my assistance; we righted her, and by sudden jerks threw out so much of the water that she would hold a man: one of them jumped in and, bailing with his two hands, succeeded in a short time in emptying her. The other native found the oars and about dark we were all three embarked. The tide having now carried us outside the breakers, I endeavored to persuade my companions in misfortune to row, but they were so benumbed with cold that they absolutely refused. I well knew that without clothing and exposed to the rigor of the air I must keep in constant exercise. Seeing, besides, that the night was advancing, and having no resource but the little strength left me, I set to work sculling and pushed off the bar, but

---

the small craft was caught in a rip and pulled away from the *Tonquin* out to sea where it capsized. Coles and Aikin were quickly lost, while Weeks and the two Sandwich Islanders managed to save themselves by righting the boat. Coles' body was never recovered. On May 26, while the *Tonquin* was still at Astoria, John Coles' effects were "disposed of" on board the ship. (Annals, p.18)

so as not to be carried out too far to sea. About midnight one of my companions died: the other threw himself upon the body of his comrade and I could not persuade him to abandon it. Daylight appeared at last; and being near the shore I headed in for it and arrived, thank God, safe and sound, through the breakers, on a sandy beach. I helped the Islander who yet gave some signs of life to get out of the boat, and we both took to the woods; but seeing that he was not able to follow me, I left him to his bad fortune and, pursuing a beaten path that I perceived, I found myself, to my great astonishment, in the course of a few hours, near the vessel."

The gentlemen who went ashore with the captain divided themselves into three parties to search for the native whom Weeks had left at the entrance of the forest; but after scouring the woods and the point of the Cape all day, they came on board in the evening without having found him.

Franchere's Journal

A Voyage to the Northwest Coast of America

Chapter Two

Setting the Foundation of the Fort

The narrative of Weeks informed us of the death of three of our companions, and we could not doubt that the five others had met a similar fate. This loss of eight of our number in two days, before we had set foot on shore, was as bad augury and was sensibly felt by all of us. In the course of so long a passage the habit of seeing each other every day, the participation of the same cares and dangers, and confinement to the same narrow limits had formed between all the passengers a connection that could not be broken, above all in a manner so sad and so unlooked for, without making us feel a void like that which is experienced in a well-regulated and loving family when it is suddenly deprived by death of the presence of one of its cherished members. We had left New York for the most part strangers to one another; but arrived at the river Columbia we were all friends, and regarded each other almost as brothers. We regretted especially the two brothers Lapensee and Joseph Nadeau: these young men had been in an especial manner recommended by their respectable parents in Canada to the care of Mr. McKay; and had acquired by their good conduct the esteem of the captain, of the crew, and of all the passengers. The brothers Lapensee were courageous and willing, never flinching in the hour of danger, and had become as good seamen as any on board. Messrs. Fox and Aikin were both highly regarded by all; the loss of Mr. Fox, above all, who was endeared to everyone by his gentlemanly behavior and affability, would have been severely regretted at any time, but it was doubly so in the present conjuncture this gentleman, who had already made a voyage to the Northwest, could have rendered important services to the captain and to the Company. The preceding days had been days of apprehension and of uneasiness; this was one of sorrow and mourning.

The following day the same gentlemen who had volunteered their services to seek for the missing islander resumed their labors, and very soon after they left us we perceived a great fire kindled at the verge of the woods, over against the ship. I was sent in a boat and arrived at the fire. It was our gentlemen who had kindled it, to restore animation to the poor Islander, whom they had at last found under the rocks, half dead with cold and fatigue, his legs swollen and his feet bleeding. We clothed him and brought him on board, where, by our care, we succeeded in restoring him to life.

Toward evening a number of the Sandwich Islanders, provided with the necessary utensils, and offerings consisting of biscuit, lard, and tobacco, went ashore to pay the last duties to their compatriot who died in Mr. Aikin's boat, on thenight of the 24th. Mr. Pillet[19] and I went with

---

[19] Francis Pillet (or Pillette) was a clerk with the Pacific Fur Co.

them and witnessed the obsequies, which took place in the manner following. Arrived at the spot where the body had been hung upon a tree to preserve it from the wolves, the natives dug a grave in the sand; then, taking down the body, and stretching it alongside the pit, they placed the biscuit under one of the arms, a piece of pork beneath the other, and the tobacco beneath the chin and the genital parts. Thus provided for the journey to the other world, the body was deposited in the grave and covered with sand and stones. All the countrymen of the dead man then knelt on either side of the grave in a double row, with their faces to the east, except one of them who officiated as priest; the latter went to the margin of the sea, and having filled his hat with water, sprinkled the two rows of islanders and recited a sort of prayer to which the others responded, nearly as we do in the litanies. That prayer ended, they rose and returned to the vessel, looking neither to the right hand nor to the left. As every one of them appeared to be familiar with the part he performed, it is more than probable that they observed, as far as circumstances permitted, the ceremonies practiced in their country on like occasions. We all returned on board about sundown.

The next day, the 27th, desirous of clearing the gangways of the live stock, we sent some men on shore to construct a pen and soon after landed about fifty hogs, committing them to the care of one of the hands. On the 30th, the long boat was manned, armed, and provisioned, and the captain, with Messrs. McKay[20] and D. Stuart[21] and some of the clerks embarked on it to ascend the river and choose an eligible spot for our trading establishment. Messrs. Ross and Pillet left at the same time, to run down south and try to obtain intelligence of Mr. Fox and his crew. In the meantime, having reached some of the goods most at hand, we commenced, with the natives who came every day to the vessel, a trade for beaver-skins, and sea-otter stones.

---

[20] Alexander McKay had traveled overland with McKenzie to the Pacific Northwest in 1792-3, He had been a partner of the North West Fur Company before retiring in 1708. He then joined the Pacific Fur Company

[21] David Stuart joined the Pacific Fur Co. in 1810 and sailed to Astoria in 1811. He helped Alexander Ross set up a trading post at Okanogan near present day Brewster, Washington.

Messrs. Ross and Pillet returned onboard on the 1st of April without having learned anything respecting Mr. Fox and his party. They did not even perceive along the beach any vestiges of the boat. The natives who occupy *Point Adams*,[22] and who are called *Clatsops*,[23] received our young gentlemen very amicably and hospitably. The captain and his companions also returned on the 4th, without having decided on a position for the establishment, finding none which appeared to them eligible. It was consequently resolved to explore the south bank, and Messrs. McDougal[24] and D. Stuart departed on that expedition the next day, promising to return by the 7th.

The 7th came and these gentlemen did not return. It rained almost all day. The day after, some natives came on board and reported that

---

[22] Named by Captain Gray 1792 to honor President John Adams.
[23] Of Chinook Family, only 200 in 1805-6 after small-pox scourge.
[24] Duncan McDougall's parents died in Canada when he was a boy. It is presumed that Duncan obtained employment with the North West Company in 1801 through two of his uncles who were partners in that firm. By 1810 McDougall had left the North West Company, joining Astor's Pacific Fur Company. He sailed on the *Tonquin* for Astoria as Astor's proxy, leaving behind two children and their mother.

Messrs. McDougal and Stuart had capsized the evening before in crossing the bay. This news at first alarmed us; and, if it had been verified, would have given the finishing blow to our discouragement. Still, as the weather was excessively bad and we did not repose entire faith in the story of the natives whom, moreover, we might not have perfectly understood, we remained in suspense till the 10th. On the morning of that day we were preparing to send some of the people in search of our two gentlemen when we perceived two large canoes, full of Indians, coming toward the vessel: they were of the *Chinook* village, which was situated at the foot of a bluff on the north side of the river, and were bringing back Messrs. McDougal and Stuart. We made known to these gentlemen the report we had heard on the 8th from the natives, and they informed us that it had been in fact well founded; that on the 7th, desirous of reaching the ship agreeably to their promise, they had quitted *Chinook* Point, in spite of the remonstrance's of the chief, Comcomly,[25] who sought to detain them by pointing out the danger to which they would expose themselves in crossing the bay in such a heavy sea as it was; that they had scarcely made more than a mile and a half before a huge wave broke over their boat and capsized it; that the Indians, aware of the danger to which they were exposed, had followed them, and that, but for their assistance, Mr. McDougal, who could not swim, would inevitably have been drowned; that after the Chinooks had kindled a large fire and dried their clothes they had been conducted by them back to their village, where the principal chief had received them with all imaginable hospitality, regaling them with every delicacy his wigwam afforded; that, in fine, if they had got back safe and sound to the vessel, it was to the timely succor and humane cares of the Indians whom we saw before us that they owed it. We liberally rewarded these generous children of the forest, and they returned home well satisfied.

This last survey was also fruitless, as Messrs. McDougal and Stuart did not find an advan-

---

[25] Lewis and Clark gave Fort Clatsop to this Chief on their departure in 1806 based upon his help and courtesy during their stay.

tageous site to build upon. But, as the captain wished to take advantage of the fine season to pursue his traffic with the natives along the N.W. coast, it was resolved to establish ourselves on *Point George,*[26] situated on the south bank, about fourteen or fifteen miles from our present anchorage, Accordingly, we embarked on the 12th, in the long-boat, to the number of twelve, furnished with tools and with provisions for a week. We landed at the bottom of a small bay, where we formed a sort of encampment. The spring, usually so tardy in this latitude, was already far advanced; the foliage was budding and the earth was clothing itself with verdure; the weather was superb and all nature smiled. We imagined ourselves in the Garden of Eden; the wild forests seemed to us delightful groves, and the leaves transformed to brilliant flowers. No doubt the pleasure of finding ourselves at the end of our voyage and liberated from the ship made things appear to us a great deal more beautiful than they really were. Be that as it may, we set ourselves to work with enthusiasm and cleared, in a

---

[26] So named In 1792 by Lieutenant Broughton of the Captain George Vancouver Expedition. It is now known as *Smith Point.*

few days, a point of land of its underbrush and of the huge trunks of pine trees that covered it, which we rolled, half-burnt, down the bank. The vessel came to moor near our encampment, and the trade went on. The natives visited us constantly and in great numbers; come to trade, others to gratify their curiosity, or to purloin some little articles if they found an opportunity. We landed the frame timbers which we had brought, ready cut for the purpose, in the vessel; and by the end of April, with the aid of the ship carpenters, John Weeks[27] and Johann Koaster,[28] we had laid the keel of a coasting schooner of about thirty tons.

---

[27] John Weeks was a member of the crew of the *Tonquin* who remained in Astoria to help with the construction of the Fort there when the *Tonquin* made its fateful voyage to the north in search of furs.

[28] Johann Koaster, a Russian and resident of New York, was hired as a carpenter with the Pacific Fur Company to help build the proposed fort at the mouth of the Columbia River. During the voyage to the northwest it was some who determined that he was not an appropriate choice for the job and was replace by crewman Henry Weeks on June 1, 1811. Koaster then sailed north on board the *Tonquin*..to his death.

Franchere's Journal

A Voyage to the Northwest Coast of America

Chapter Three

Voyage up the Columbia

The Indians having informed us that above certain rapids there was an establishment of white men, we doubted not that it was a trading post of the North West Company; and to make sure of it, we procured a large canoe and a guide and set out on the 2d of May, Messrs. McKay, R. Stuart,[29] Montigny,[30] and I, with a sufficient

---

[29] Robert Stuart was a nephew of David Stuart mentioned above. He was employed with the Pacific Fur Company and arrived in Astoria aboard the aboard the *Tonquin*.

[30] French-Canadian Ovide de Montigny had an eleven year career in the fur trade on the Pacific slopes. de Montigny signed on with the Pacific Fur Company as a voyager in Montreal on July 23, 1810 and then started on his way to New York City. On his way, on August 3, 1810, he joined Gabriel Franchere and Alexander McKay at Whitehall, N.Y., and sailed to the mouth of the Columbia arriving March 22, 1811. Alexander McKay selected Ovide to go north on the *Tonquin*, but, as Ovide was prone to seasickness, he declined, an act which saved his life. He went on to Fort

number of hands. We first passed a lofty head land that seemed at a distance to be detached from the main, and to which we gave the name of *Tongue Point*.[31] Here the river gains a width of some nine or ten miles and keeps it for about twelve miles up. The left bank, which we were coasting, being concealed by little low islands, we encamped for the night on one of them, at the village of *Wahkaykum*,[32] to which our guide belonged.

We continued our journey on the 3d: the river narrows considerably at about thirty miles from its mouth, and is obstructed with islands which are thickly covered with the willow, poplar, alder, and ash. These islands are, without exception,

Okanagan in 1811, to the Thompson River with David Stuart in 1812, and was in Fort Okanagan in 1814 at the end of his one year contract with North West Company. On April 13 of that year, he gave a letter, written to his brother, to be delivered by the departing Franchere who did not see a future for himself in the North West Company which had acquired the Pacific Fur Company. de Montigny possibly continued on in the area, joining Hudson's Bay Company at amalgamation in 1821, until 1822-23 when he picked up his pay in Montreal. In 1843, Ovide appears to be living at the Ile Perrot, district of Montreal with his wife, Josephte Fagnon and their son Narcisse. (B.C. Metis)

[31] *Point Adams, "Tongue" Point* was so previously named after the shape of the Point

[32] A Chinookan Tribe, near Pillar Rock, above Gray's Bay. In 1805 Lewis and Clark estimated their number at 200.

uninhabited and uninhabitable, being nothing but swamps, and entirely overflowed in the months of June and July; as we understood from *Coalpo*, our guide, who appeared to be an intelligent man. In proportion as we advanced, we saw the high mountains capped with snow which form the chief and majestic feature, though a-stern one, of the banks of the Columbia for some distance from its mouth, recede, and give place to a country of moderate elevation and rising amphitheatrically from the margin of the stream. The river narrows to a mile or thereabouts; the forest is less dense, and patches of green prairie are seen. We passed a large village on the south bank, called *Kreluit*, above which is a fine forest of oaks; and encamped for the night on a low point, at the foot of an isolated rock about one hundred and fifty feet high. This rock appeared to me remarkable on account of its situation, reposing in the midst of a low and swampy ground, as if it had been dropped from the clouds, and seeming to have no connection with the neighboring mountains. On a cornice or shelving projection about thirty feet from its base the natives of the adjacent villages deposit their dead in canoes; and it is the same rock to which, for this reason, Lieutenant Broughton gave the name of *Mount Coffin*.[33]

On the 4th, in the morning, we arrived at a large village of the same name as that which we had passed the evening before, Kreluit, and we landed to obtain information respecting a considerable stream which here discharges into the Columbia, and respecting its resources for the hunter and trader in furs. It comes from the north and is called *Cowilitzk*[34] by the natives. Mr. McKay embarked with Mr. de Montigny and two Indians in a small canoe to examine the course of this river a certain distance up. On entering the stream they saw a great number of birds which they took at first for turkeys, so much they resembled them, but which were only a kind of carrion eagles, vulgarly called *turkey buzzards*. We were not a little astonished to see Mr. de Montigny return on foot and alone; he soon informed us of the reason: having ascended

---

[33] A promontory in now Longview, WA then used as an Indian Cemetery

[34] The Cowelishee of Lewis and Clark, now the Cowlitz River.

the Cowilitzk about a mile and a half, on rounding a bend of the stream they suddenly came in
view of about twenty canoes, full of Indians, who
had made a rush upon them with the most
frightful yells; the two natives and the guide who
conducted their little canoe retreated with the ut-
most precipitancy, but seeing that they would be
overtaken they stopped short and begged Mr.
McKay to fire upon the approaching savages,
which he, being well acquainted with the Indian
character from the time he accompanied Sir Alexander Mackenzie, and having met with similar
occurrences before, would by no means do; but
displayed a friendly sign to the astonished natives and invited them to land for an amicable
talk; to which they immediately assented. Mr.
McKay had sent Mr. de Montigny to procure
some tobacco and a pipe in order to strike a
peace with these barbarians. The latter then returned to Mr. McKay with the necessary articles
and in the evening the party came back to our
camp, which we had fixed between the villages.
We were then informed that the Indians whom

Mr. McKay had met were at war with the *Kreluits*.[35] It was impossible, consequently, to close our eyes all night; the natives passing and re-passing continually from one village to the other, making fearful cries, and coming every minute to solicit us to discharge our firearms; all to frighten their enemies and let them see that they were on their guard.

On the 5th, in the morning, we paid a visit to the hostile camp; and those savages, who had never seen white men, regarded us with curiosity and astonishment, lifting the legs of our trousers and opening our shirts to see if the skin of our bodies resembled that of our faces and hands. We remained some time with them to make pro-posals of peace; and having ascertained that this warlike demonstration originated in a trifling of-fense on the part of the Kreluits, we found them well disposed to arrange matters in an amicable fashion. After having given them, therefore, some looking-glasses, beads, knives, tobacco, and other trifles, we quitted them and pursued our way.

---

[35] Skiloots to the Lewis and Clark Expedition

Having passed a deserted village and then several islands, we came in sight of a noble mountain on the north, about twenty miles distant, all covered with snow, contrasting remarkably with the dark foliage of the forests at its base, and probably the same which was seen by Broughton, and named by him *Mount St. Helen.*[36] We pulled against a strong current all this day and at evening our guide made us enter a little river, on the bank of which we found a good camping place under a grove of oaks and in the midst of odoriferous wild flowers, where we passed a night more tranquil than that which had preceded it.

On the morning of the 6th we ascended this small stream and soon arrived at a large village called Thlacalama,[37] the chief whereof, who was a young and handsome man, was called Keasseno,[38] and was a relative of our guide. The situation of this village is the most charming that can be, being built on the little river that we had ascended, and indeed at its navigable head, being

---

[36] So named in October, 1792 by Lieutenant Broughton in honor of Lord St. Helen, British Ambassador to Madrid.

[37] A village built on both sides of a small stream.

[38] Chief of the Willamettes and brother-in-law of guide Coalpo.

here but a torrent with numerous cascades leap-
ing from rock to rock in their descent to the
deep, limpid water, which then flows through a
beautiful prairie enameled with odoriferous flowers of all colors and studded with superb groves
of oak. The freshness and beauty of this spot,
which Nature seemed to have taken pleasure in
adorning and enriching with her most precious
gifts, contrasted in a striking manner with the
indigence and uncleanliness of its inhabitants;
and I regretted that it had not fallen to the lot of
civilized men. I was wrong no doubt: it is just
that those should be most favored by their common mother who are least disposed to pervert
her gifts or to give the preference to advantages
which are factitious and often very frivolous.

We quitted with regret this charming spot and
soon came to another large village which our
guide informed us was called Kathlapootle,[39] and

---

[39] Lewis and Clark visited 1806, 14 wooded houses, 900 Indians.
Radiocarbon dating indicates that this village was located at this
site in 1450 AD. Ceramic trade goods indicate that the site was
abandoned in 1834 AD. Archaeologists have located 11 house
depressions on the surface in two rows on a ridge running parallel to Lake River. The largest house depression is 200 feet by 45
feet, the smallest being 60 feet by 30 feet. At least four were
divided into compartments as Lewis and Clark had described.

was situated at the confluence of a small stream that seemed to flow down from the mountain covered with snow, which we had seen the day before: this river is called Cowilkt. We coasted a pretty island, well timbered and high enough above the level of the Columbia to escape inundation in the freshets, and arrived at two villages called Maltnabah.[40] We then passed the confluence of the river Wallamat or Willamet[41], above which the tide ceases to be felt in the Columbia. Our guide informed us that ascending this river about a day's journey there was a considerable falls, beyond which the country abounded in deer, elk, bear, beaver, and otter. But here at the spot where there were the oaks and poplar which line both banks of the river, the green and flowery prairies discerned through the trees, and the mountains discovered in the distance offer to the eye of the observer who loves the beauties of simple nature a prospect the most lovely and enchanting. We encamped for the night on the edge of one of these fine prairies.

On the 7th we passed several low islands and

---

[40] White men later pronounced it "Maltnomah."
[41] Now known as the Willamette.

soon discovered *Mount Hood*,[42] a high mountain capped with snow, so named by Lieutenant Broughton; and *Mount Washington*,[43] another snowy summit, so called by Lewis and Clark. The prospect which the former had before his eyes at this place appeared to him so charming that, landing upon a point to take possession of the country in the name of King George, he named it *Point Belle Vue*.[44] At two o'clock we passed *Point Vancouver*,[45] the highest reached by Broughton. The width of the river diminishes considerably above this point, and we began very soon to encounter shoals of sand and gravel; a sure indication that we were nearing the rapids. We encamped that evening under a ledge of rocks, descending almost to the water's edge.

The next day, the 8th, we did not proceed far before we encountered a very rapid current. Soon after, we saw a hut of Indians engaged in fishing, where we stopped to breakfast. We found here an

---

[42] Named for Lord Hood, later Lord Bridport, an English Admiral.

[43] Franchere's Mount Washington (7,800 feet) is not visible from the Columbia River. It may have been Mount Jefferson (10,495 feet).

[44] Either Kelly Point (?) or as now named on Sauvie Island.(?)

[45] Point Vancouver is in reality twenty miles further up river.

old blind man, who gave us a cordial reception. Our guide said that he was a white man, and that his name was *Soto*. We learned from the mouth of the old man himself that he was the son of a Spaniard[46] who had been wrecked at the

---

[46]Soto's father was said to have been Konapee, shipwrecked in 1725. In about 1725, Clatsops discover shipwrecked sailors whom they call Tlehonnipts (those who drift ashore) on a beach near Satsop Spit, which was located on the southern (Oregon) side of the mouth of the Columbia River. One of the sailors will be called Konapee the Iron Maker. They are probably the first European residents of the Pacific Northwest and will marry into Native American tribes in the region. The men may be Spanish or Mexican sailors engaged in the trade between Manila and Mexico. Clatsop oral tradition records that an old woman from the village of Ne-Ahkstow, about two miles south of Clatsop Spit, encountered a whale or an immense canoe with trees growing out of it. A bear-like creature emerged and frightened the woman who rushed home to alert the village. Clatsops found two men with beards who possessed metals unknown to them. Somehow their ship caught fire, but the Indians were able to recover iron, copper, and brass. Word spread quickly among the tribes of the coast and interior and all wanted to take possession of these strangers as slaves. Ultimately the Clatsops agreed to yield up one man to the Willapas on the north side of the Columbia River while they retained one. The Clatsop slave was put to work converting metals into useful tools and he earned the name Konapee the Iron Maker. As he demonstrated his utility to the tribe he was granted more freedom. The area where he worked was called Konapee. Explorer James Cook, the first European recorded to have visited the Northwest, noticed in 1778 that the natives seemed familiar with iron implements and weapons. (HistoryLink Washington State Library)

mouth of the river; that a part of the crew on this occasion got safe ashore, but were all massacred by the Clatsops with the exception of four, who were spared and who married native women; that these four Spaniards, of whom his father was one, disgusted with the savage life, attempted to reach a settlement of their own nation toward the south, but had never been heard of since; and that when his father, with his companions, left the country, he himself was yet quite young. These good people having regaled us with fresh salmon, we left them and arrived very soon at a rapid opposite an island, named *Strawberry Island*[47] by Captains Lewis and Clark in 1806. We left our men at a large village to take care of the canoe and baggage ; and following our guide, after walking about two hours in a beaten path we came to the foot of the fall, where we amused ourselves for some time with shooting the seals, which were here in abundance, and in watching the Indians taking salmon below the cataract in their scoop-nets, from stages erected for that purpose over the eddies. A chief, a young

---

[47]McArthur notes: Strawberry Island so named by Lewis and Clark because of all the vines is now Hamilton Island.

man of fine person and a good mien, came to us, followed by some twenty others, and invited us to his wigwam: we accompanied him, had roasted salmon for supper, and some mats were spread for our night's repose.

The next morning, having ascertained that there was no trading post[48] near the Falls, and Coalpo absolutely refusing to proceed farther, alleging that the natives of the villages beyond were his enemies and would not fail to kill him[49] if they had him in their power, we decided to return to the encampment. Having, therefore, distributed some presents to our host (I mean the young chief with whom we had supped and lodged) and to some of his followers, and procured a supply of fresh salmon for the return voyage, we re-embarked and reached the camp on the 14th without accidents or incidents worth relating.

---

[48] McDougall took false comfort in the notion that there was no competition on the Columbia River. This assumption would be disproved with the arrival of David Thompson of the North West Company on July 15.

[49] On October 24, 1805, The two Indian Chief guides told Lewis and Clark as they traveled downriver, the same thing as did Coalpo in guiding this expedition upriver. The Indians below and above the Great Falls apparently did not get along too well.

Franchere's Journal

A Voyage to the Northwest Coast of America

Chapter Four
Fort Astoria Completed

Having built a warehouse (62 feet by 20)to put under cover the articles we were to receive from the ship, we were busily occupied from the 16th to the 30th in stowing away the goods and other effects intended for the establishment.

The ship, which had been detained by circumstances much longer than had been anticipated, left her anchorage at last on the 1st of June and dropped down to *Baker Bay*, there to wait for a favorable wind to get out of the river. As she was to coast along the north and enter all the harbors in order to procure as many furs as possible, and to touch at the Columbia River before she finally left these seas for the United States, it was unanimously resolved among the partners that Mr. McKay should join the cruise, as well to aid the captain as to obtain correct information in regard to the commerce with the natives on that coast.[50]

Mr. McKay selected Messrs. J. Lewis[51] and O. de Montigny to accompany him; but the latter having represented that the sea made him sick, was excused; and Mr. McKay shipped in his place a young man named Louis Brusle to serve him in the capacity of domestic, being one of the young Canadian sailors. I had the good fortune not to be chosen for this disastrous voyage, thanks to my having made myself useful at the establishment. Mr. Mumford (the second mate) owed the same happiness to the incompatibility of his disposition with that of the captain; he had permission to remain, and engaged with the

---

[50] Most of the cargo that was intended for Fort Astoria was not unloaded during the two and a half months the *Tonquin* lay in the Columbia. It was intended to be unloaded upon its return.

[51] James Lewis was a clerk with the Pacific Fur Company who was killed aboard the *Tonquin* during its furring expedition in 1811.

Company in place of Mr. Aikin as coaster, and in command of the schooner.[52]

On the 5th of June the ship got out to sea, with a good wind. We continued in the mean time to labor without intermission at the completion of the storehouse, and in the erection of a dwelling for ourselves and a powder magazine. These buildings were constructed of hewn logs, and in the absence of boards were tightly covered and roofed with cedar bark. The natives of both sexes visited us more frequently, and formed a pretty considerable camp near the establishment.

On the 15th some natives from up the river brought us two strange Indians,[53] a man and a

---

[52] Franchere notes: This schooner was found too small for this purpose. Mr. Astor had no idea of the danger to be met at the mouth of the Columbia or he would have ordered the frame of vessel of at least one hundred tons. The frame shipped in New York were used in the construction of this one only.

[53] Bancroft notes: It was afterwards ascertained that these were women though one of them was dressed as a man, thinking in that garb she would meet with greater respect. They were remarkable characters. There sort of uncivilized mountebanks, and practiced skillfully and successfully most of the cheats known to white men and savages. Among the Natives they professed great influence with the fur traders, which might secure the great blessings. On the journey up the river, which subsequently took place, Ross was unable to account "for the cordial reception they

woman. They were not attired like the savages on the river Columbia, but wore long robes of dressed deer-skin, with leggings and moccasins in the fashion of the tribes to the east of the Rocky Mountains. We put questions to them in various Indian dialects, but they did not understand us. They showed us a letter addressed to "Mr. John Stuart,[54] Fort Estekatadene,[55] New Caledonia." Mr. Pillet then addressing them in the Kaisteneaux language,[56] they answered, although they appeared not to understand it perfectly. Notwithstanding, we learned from them that they had been sent by a Mr. Finnan McDonald,[57] a clerk in the service of the North West Company, and who had a post on a river which

---

received from the Natives who loaded them for their good tidings with the most valuable items they possessed..."

[54] John Stuart was a longtime Canadian fur trader. He had built a fort west of the Rocky Mountains, possibly the Fraser River area, where he remained until 1811 relocating to the Columbia River area. In 1812 he joined the operation at Astoria where he worked until 1814.

[55] Nothing is known about this fort. Probably in British Columbia.

[56] Language of Cree Indians who live primarily in Canada.

[57] Finnan McDonald was chief clerk under David Thompson of the North West Company at various places on the Saskatchewan, in the Rocky Mountains and upon the head waters of the Columbia. (1806-12). Thompson and McDonald had one post on Lake Pend d'Oreille, two on the Kootenay, and another on the Spokane.

they called *Spokan*; that having lost their way, they had followed the course of the Tacousah-Tesseh (the Indian name of the Columbia) that when they arrived at the Falls the natives made them understand that there were white men at the mouth of the river; and not doubting that the person to whom the letter was addressed would be found there, they had come to deliver it.

We kept these messengers for some days, and having drawn from them important information respecting the country in the interior west of the Mountains, we decided to send an expedition thither under the command of Mr. David Stuart; and the 15th of July was fixed for its departure.[58] All was in fact ready on the appointed day and

---

[58] John Stuart's Journal relates the follow concerning these two visitors: June 14, Kemakiah, chief of the Clatsops, informed the Americans that two Indians from far in the interior were at the village of Cathlamets. He also gave a long story on the reasons for their journey, but not a word could be understood. The following day, the two Indians (a man and a woman), arrived in a dugout with seven other natives, mostly Clatsops. He delivered a letter addressed to Mr. Stuart, at Fort Estekakamac. Mr. MacDougall opened it. It was dated from Fort Flathead, on April 5. Neither its contents, nor the questions which were asked of the Indian, could shed light on the cause of their voyage. But it was soon realized that this foreigner spoke the language of Kaisténaux, which lead to suspicion that he was a half-breed of the nations of the north-west and a spy for the company of the same name. (McTavish would come as a North West Company spy, later! ed.)

we were about to load the canoes, when toward midday we saw a large canoe with a flag displayed at her stern rounding the point which we called *Tongue Point*. We knew not who it could be; for we did not so soon expect our own party, who (the reader will remember) were to cross the continent by the route which Captains Lewis and Clark had followed in 1805, and to winter for that purpose somewhere on the Missouri. We were soon relieved of our uncertainty by the arrival of the canoe, which touched shore at a little wharf that we had built to facilitate the landing of goods from the vessel. The flag she bore was the British, and her crew was composed of eight Canadian boatmen or voyageurs. A well dressed man, who appeared to be the commander, was the first to leap ashore, and addressing us without ceremony, said that his name was David Thompson[59] and that he was one of the partners

---

[59] During Thompson's 1811 voyage down the Columbia River he camped at the junction with the Snake River on July 9, 1811, and erected a pole and a notice claiming the country for Britain and stating the intention of the North West Co. to build a trading post at the site. This notice was found later that year by Astorians looking to establish an inland fur post. On July 14 he reached the partially constructed Fort Astoria at the mouth of the Columbia, arriving two months after the Pacific Fur Co. ship, the *Tonquin*.

of the North West Company. We invited him to our quarters, which were at one end of the warehouse, the dwelling-house not being yet completed. After the usual civilities had been extended to our visitor, Mr. Thompson said that he had crossed the Continent during the preceding season; but that the desertion of a portion of his men had compelled him to winter at the base of the Rocky Mountains, at the head waters of the Columbia. In the spring he had built a canoe, the materials for which he had brought

---

Thompson was one of the most interesting and remarkable men of the fur-trading coterie. Born in London in 1770, and educated at Christ's hospital, he came to America in 1789 as an employee of Hudson's Bay Company. He was very interested in science, and during his extensive travels made meteorological and astrological observations. The company by whom he was initially employed discouraged geographical pursuits. Thompson therefore went over to the North West Company (1797) as affording more scope for his talents. During the winter of 1797-98 he visited the Mandan Indians, on the Missouri, and the following summer examined the sources of the Mississippi. In 1801 he had pushed his explorations to the foot of the Rocky Mountains, whither in 1806 he sought for the waters of the Columbia. During the next four years he collected furs and explored the upper Columbia, built several posts, and reaping a rich harvest among the tribes hitherto unexploited. After his failure to seize the mouth of the Columbia for the British, Thompson went back to his Columbia posts but finally abandoned the upper country in 1812. He lived in Lower Canada until his death in 1857, occupied in surveys of boundary lines and astronomical pursuits. His last years were spent in poverty and neglect. (Early Western Travels...).

with him across the mountains, and had come down the river to our establishment. He added that the wintering partners had resolved to abandon all their trading posts west of the mountains, not to enter into competition with us, provided our company would engage not to encroach upon their commerce on the east side: and to support what he said, produced a letter to that effect, addressed by the wintering partners to the chief of their house in Canada, the Hon. *William McGillivray*[60].

Mr. Thompson kept a regular journal, and traveled, I thought, more like a geographer than a fur-trader. He was provided with a sextant, chronometer, and barometer, and during a week's sojourn which he made at our place had an opportunity to make several astronomical observations. He recognized the two Indians who had

---

[60] William McGillivray was a "Nor'Wester" who had been in the employ since its formation, and served his apprenticeship in the field. In 1787-88 he was in charge of the post on English River, and in 1790 became one of the wintering partners. Upon the death of Simon McTavish, McGillivray succeeded to the position of chief agent of the house at Montreal, frequently coming up to meet "winterers" at the rendezvous at Fort William which was named in his honor. In 1821 he signed the agreements for union with Hudson's Bay Company and soon after returned to Scotland where he died about 1825.

brought the letter addressed to Mr. J. Stuart, and told us that they were two women, one of whom had dressed herself as a man to travel with more security. The description which he gave us of the interior of the country was not calculated to give us a very favorable idea of it, and did not perfectly accord with that of our two Indian guests. We persevered, however, in the resolution we had taken of sending an expedition thither; and on the 2d Mr. D. Stuart set out, accompanied by Messrs. Pillet, Ross, McClellan and de Montigny, with four Canadian voyageurs and the two Indian women, and in company with Mr. Thompson and his crew. The wind being favorable, the little flotilla hoisted sail and was soon out of our sight.

The natives, who till then had surrounded us in great numbers,[61] began to withdraw, and very soon we saw no more of them. At first we attributed their absence to the want of furs to trade with; but we soon learned that they acted in that

---

[61] Spaulding notes: "Numerically, the settlement could hardly match with its neighbors: nearly 1,000 braves - 214 Chinooks, 180 Clatsops, 234 of the remote Chehalis to the north, and 200 Tillamook's to the South."

manner from another motive. One of the second-
ary chiefs, who had formed a friendship for Mr.
R. Stuart, informed him that seeing us reduced
in number by the expedition lately sent off, they
had formed the design of surprising us, to take
our lives and plunder the post. We hastened,
therefore, to put ourselves in the best possible
state of defense. The dwelling house was raised,
parallel to the warehouse; we cut a great quantity of pickets in the forest and formed a square,
with palisades in front and rear, of about 90 feet
by 120; the warehouse, built on the edge of a ra-
vine, formed one flank, the dwelling house and
shops the other; with a little bastion at each an-
gle north and south, on which were mounted
four small cannon. The whole was finished in six
days, and had a sufficiently formidable aspect to
deter the Indians from attacking us; and for
greater surety we organized a guard for day and
night.

Toward the end of the month a large assem-
blage of Indians from the neighborhood of the
Strait of Juan de Fuca and Gray's Harbor formed
a great camp on Baker's Bay for the ostensible

object of fishing for sturgeon. It was bruited among these Indians that the *Tonquin* had been destroyed on the Coast, and Mr. McKay (or the chief trader, as they called him) and all the crew massacred by the natives. We did not give credence to this rumor. Some days after, other Indians from Gray's Harbor, called *Tchikeylis*,[62] confirmed what the first had narrated and even gave us, as far as we could judge by the little we knew of their language, a very circumstantial detail of the affair, so that, without wholly convincing us, it did not fail to make a painful impression on our minds and keep us in an excited state of feeling as to the truth of the report. The Indians of the Bay looked fiercer and more war-like than those of our neighborhood; so we re-doubled our vigilance and performed a regular daily drill to accustom ourselves to the use of arms.

To the necessity of securing ourselves against an attack on the part of the natives was joined that of obtaining a stock of provisions for the winter: those which we had received from the

---

[62] Chehalis (Tchikeylis, Shahalas) is a collective term for the Shalisban tribes of the coast of Washington, where a large country takes its name.

vessel were very quickly exhausted, and from the commencement of the month of July we were forced to depend upon fish. Not having brought hunters with us, we had to rely for venison on the precarious hunt of one of the natives who had not abandoned us when the rest of his countrymen retired. This man brought us from time to time a very lean and very dry doe-elk, for which we had to pay, notwithstanding, very dear. The ordinary price of a stag was a blanket, a knife, some tobacco, powder and ball, besides supplying our hunter with a musket. This dry meat and smoke-dried fish constituted our daily food, and that in very insufficient quantity for hardworking men. We had no bread, and vegetables, of course, were quite out of the question. In a word, our fare was not sumptuous. Those who accommodated themselves best to our mode of living were the Sandwich Islanders: salmon and elk were to them exquisite viands.

On the 9th of August a number of Chinooks visited us, bringing a strange Indian who had, they said, something interesting to communicate. This savage told us, in fact, that he had been en-

gaged with ten more of his countrymen by a *Captain Ayres*[63] to hunt seals on the islands in *Sir
Francis Drake's Bay*, where these animals are
very numerous, with a promise of being taken
home and paid for their services; the captain had
left them on the islands to go southwardly and
purchase provisions, he said, of the Spaniards of
Monterey in California; but he had never returned: and they, believing that he had been
wrecked, had embarked in a skiff which he had
left them and had reached the main land, from
which they were not far distant; but their skiff
was shattered to pieces in the surf, and they had
saved themselves by swimming. Believing that
they were not far from the river Columbia, they
had followed the shore, living, on the way, upon
shell-fish and frogs; at last they arrived among
strange Indians who, far from receiving them
kindly, had killed eight of them and made the
rest prisoners; but the Kelemoux,[64] a neighboring

---

[63] Some think this story is in reference to Captain George W.
Ayres of the *Mercury*, who hunted furs under agreement with
Baranov in Sitka in 1808. Leaving Sitka in May, the share of his
company was 1040 skins.
[64] Now known as the Tillamook Indians

tribe to the Clatsops, hearing that they were captives, had ransomed them.

These facts must have occurred in March or April, 1811. The Indian who gave us an account of them appeared to have a great deal of intelligence and knew some words of the English language. He added that he had been at the Russian trading post at Chitka,(Sitka) that he had visited the coast of California, the Sandwich Islands and even China.

About this time old Comcomly sent to Astoria for Mr. Stuart and me to come and cure him of a swelled throat, which, he said, afflicted him sorely. As it was late in the day we postponed till tomorrow going to cure the chief of the Chinooks; and it was well we did; for the same evening the wife of the Indian who had accompanied us in our voyage to the Falls sent us word that Comcomly was perfectly well, the pretended tonsillitis being only a pretext to get us in his power. This timely advice kept us at home.

Franchere's Journal

A Voyage to the Northwest Coast of America

Chapter Five
Desertion and Pursuit

On the 26th of September our house was fin-
nished, and we took possession of it. The mason
work had at first caused us some difficulty; but
at last, not being able to make lime for want of
limestone, we employed blue clay as a substitute
for mortar. This dwelling-house was sufficiently
spacious to hold all our company, and we had
distributed it in the most convenient manner
that we could. It comprised a sitting, a dining
room, some lodging or sleeping rooms, and an
apartment for the men and officers, all under the
same roof. We also completed a shop for the
blacksmith, who till that time had worked in the
open air.

The schooner, the construction of which had necessarily languished for want of an adequate force at the shipyard, was finally launched on the 2d of October and named the *Dolly*[65] with the formalities usual on such occasions. I was on that day at *Young's Bay*,[66] where I saw the ruins of the quarters erected by *Captains Lewis and Clark*, in 1805-06; they were but piles of rough, unhewn logs, overgrown with parasite creepers.

On the evening of the 5th, Messrs. Pillet and McLellan[67] arrived from the party of Mr. David Stuart in a canoe manned by two of his men. They brought as passengers Mr. *Regis Bruguier*,

---

[65] The *Dolly*, named for Astor's wife, having made two or three trips up the Colombia River, she was condemned, and laid aside altogether as useless. She was quickly rechristened the *Jane*. Henry, capitalizing on Jane's boredom with the long ocean voyage, offered her what he referred to in his journal as "protection;" Donald McTavish had brought Jane Burns, a barmaid from Portsmouth, to Astoria on the *Isaac Todd* and, after a few sharp words, contented himself with the Chinook consort incongruously known as Mrs. Clapp. Chief Comcomly's son, even more electrified, rushed emissaries across the river with an offer of one hundred choice sea-otter skins for Jane's plump hand. With the downfall of the Astor enterprise that built her, *Dolly* fell into the hands of the British who renamed her the *Columbia*. After a few years she was taken to California and dismantled.

[66] Young's Bay is a body of water just west of Astoria. The bay was named by Lieutenant Broughton after a fellow naval officer.

[67] Donald McLellan was clerk with Pacific Fur Co. who arrived on the *Tonquin*.

whom I had known in Canada as a respectable country merchant, and an Iroquois[68] family. Mr. Bruguier[69] had been a trader among the Indians on the *Saskatchewine River*, where he had lost his outfit: he had since turned trapper and had come into this region to hunt beaver, being provided with traps and other needful implements.

The report which these gentlemen gave of the interior was highly satisfactory: they had found the climate salubrious, and had been well received by the natives. The latter possessed a great number of horses and Mr. Stuart had purchased several of these animals at a low price. Ascending the river, they had come to a pretty stream, which the natives called Okenakane.[70] Mr. Stuart had resolved to establish his post on the bank of this river, and having erected a log-house he thought best to send back the above named persons, retaining with him for the winter only Messrs. Ross and de Montigny, and two

---

[68] A member of a federation of Indian tribes of New York state.

[69] Mr. Bruguier was what was known as a "free trapper", one who wandered through the wilderness trapping and trading on his own account. Most of these were Canadians or half-breeds.

[70] A tribe of Indians whose traditional territory is located in northern Washington State and Southern British Columbia.

men. Meanwhile, the season being come when the Indians quit the sea-shore and the banks of the Columbia to retire into the woods and establish their winter quarters along the small streams and rivers, we began to find ourselves short of provisions, having received no supplies from them for some time. It was therefore determined that Mr. R. Stuart should set out in the schooner with Mr. Mumford for the threefold purpose of obtaining all the provisions they could, cutting oaken staves for the use of the cooper, and trading with the Indians up the river. They left with this design on the 12th. At the end of 5 days Mr. Mumford returned in a canoe of Indians. This man having wished to assume the command and to order (in the style of Captain Thorn) the person who had engaged him to obey, had been sent back in consequence to Astoria.

On the 10th of November we discovered that three of our people had absconded, viz., P. D. Jeremie[71] and the two Belleaux, They had leave

---

[71] Jeremie arrived as a voyager of Pacific Fur Co. on the *Tonquin*, he was a boat-builder. The two Belleaux had also arrived on the Tonquin.

to go out shooting for two days, and carried off with them firearms and ammunition and a handsome light Indian canoe. As soon as their flight was known, having procured a large canoe of the Chinooks we embarked, Mr. Matthews[72] and I, with five natives, to pursue them, with orders to proceed as far as the Falls if necessary. On the 9th, having ascended the river to a place called *Oak Point* ,[73] we overlooked the schooner lying at anchor while Mr. Stuart was taking in a load of staves and hoop-poles. Mr. Farnham[74] joined our party, as well as one of the hands, and thus reinforced we pursued our way, journeying day and night and stopping at every Indian village to make inquiries and offer a reward for the appre-

---

[72] Matthews enlisted in the Astoria expedition as a clerk. He married the daughter of a Clatsop Chief. Their daughter, Ellen, born in 1815, is the first recorded white child born in Oregon.

[73] Oak Point is a well known land mark on the Columbia River so named by Lieutenant Broughton (1792) who saw oaks at this place. It was on the south bank of the river nearly opposite the upper end of Grim's Island. Oak Point is about forty miles up the Columbia from its mouth. Curry noted: Oak Point was the location of the first American settlement on the Columbia River. Captain Smith of the ship *Albatross* of Boston, in the spring of 1810 cleared, fenced and cultivated and a piece of land, but the annual freshit of the river submerged his improvements and caused him to abandon the project.

[74] Russell Farnham was a clerk of Pacific Fur Co. who arrived on the *Tonquin.*

hension of our runaways. Having reached the Falls without finding any trace of them, and our provisions giving out, we retraced our steps and arrived on the 16th at Oak Point, where we found Mr. Stuart ready to quit.

Meanwhile, the natives of the vicinity informed us that they had seen the marks of shoes imprinted on the sand at the confluence of a small stream in the neighborhood. We got three small canoes carrying two persons each, and having ascertained that the information was correct, after searching the environs during a part of the 17th we ascended the small stream as far as the high lands which are seen from *Oak Point*, and which lie about eight or nine miles south of it.

The space between these high lands and the ridge crowned with oaks on the bank of the Columbia is a low and swampy land, cut up by an infinity of little channels. Toward evening we returned on our path to regain the schooner; but instead of taking the circuitous way of the river, by which we had come, we made for Oak Point by the most direct route through these channels; but night coming on, we lost ourselves. Our situation became the most disagreeable that can be imagined. Being unable to find a place where we could land, on account of the morass, we were obliged to continue rowing, or rather turning round, in this species of labyrinth, constantly kneeling in our little canoes, which any unlucky movement would infallibly have caused to upset. It rained in torrents and was dark as pitch. At last, after having wandered about during a considerable part of the night we succeeded in gaining the edge of the mainland. Leaving there our canoes because we could not drag them (as we attempted) through the forest, we crossed the woods in the darkness, tearing ourselves with the brush, and reached the schooner at about two in the morning, benumbed with cold and exhausted with fatigue.

The 18th was spent in getting in the remainder of the lading of the little vessel, and on the morning of the 19th we raised anchor and dropped it abreast of the Kreluit village, where some of the Indians offering to aid us in the search after our deserters, Mr. Stuart put Mr. Farnham and me on shore to make another attempt. We passed that day in drying our clothes and the next day embarked in a canoe with one Kreluit-man and a squaw, and ascended the river before described as entering the Columbia at this place.

We soon met a canoe of natives who informed us that our runaways had been made prisoners by the chief of a tribe which dwells upon the banks of the Willamette River, and which they called Cathlanaminimin. We kept on and en-camped on a beach of sand opposite Deer Island.

There we passed a night almost as disagreeab-le as that of the 17th-18th. We had lighted a fire and contrived a shelter of mats; but there came on presently a violent gust of wind, accompanied with a heavy rain: our fire was put out, our mats were carried away, and we could neither rekindle the one nor find the others: so that we had to re-main all night exposed to the fury of the storm. As soon as it was day we re-embarked and set ourselves to paddling with all our might to warm ourselves. In the evening we arrived near the village where our deserters were and saw one of them on the skirts of it. We proceeded to the hut of the chief where we found all three, more inclined to follow us than to remain as slaves among these barbarians. We passed the night in the chief's lodge, not without some fear and some precaution; this chief having the reputation of being a wicked man and capable of violating the rights of parties. He was a man of high stature and a good mien, and proud in proportion, as we discovered by the chilling and haughty manner in which he received us. Farnham and I agreed to keep watch alternately, but this arrangement was superfluous as neither of us could sleep a wink for the infernal thumping and singing made by the medicine men all night long by a dying native. I had an opportunity of seeing the sick man make his last will and testament: having caused to be brought to him whatever he had that was most precious, his bracelets of copper, his bead necklace, his bow and arrows and quiver, his nets, his lines, his spear, his pipe, &c., he distributed the whole to his most inti-mate friends, with a promise on their part to re-store them, if he recovered.

On the 22d, after a great deal of talk and infinite quibbling on the part of the chief[75], we agreed with him for the ransom of our men. I had visited very lodge in the village and found but few of the young men, the greater part having gone on a fishing excursion; knowing, therefore, that the chief could not be supported by his warriors, I was resolved not to be imposed upon, and as I knew where the firearms of the fugitives had been deposited I would have them at all hazards; but we were obliged to give him all our blankets, amounting to eight, a brass kettle, a hatchet, a small pistol, much out of order, a powder-horn, and some rounds of ammunition: with these articles placed in a pile before him we demanded the men's clothing, the three fowling-pieces, and their canoe, which he had caused to be hidden in the woods. Nothing but our firmness compelled him to accept the articles offered in exchange; but at last, with great reluctance, he closed the bargain and suffered us to depart in the evening with the prisoners and the property.

---

[75] Dodilcham, sometimes spelled Tootichum.

We all five (including the three deserters) embarked in the large canoe, leaving our Kreluit and his wife to follow in the other, and proceeded as far as the Cowlitzk, where we camped. The next day we pursued our journey homeward, only stopping at the Kreluit village to get some provisions, and soon entered the group of islands which crowd the river above Gray's Bay. On one of these we stopped to amuse ourselves with shooting some ducks, and meanwhile a smart breeze springing up, we split open a double-rush mat (which had served as a bag) to make a sail, and having cut a forked sapling for a mast, shipped a few boulders to stay the foot of it and spread our canvass to the wind. We soon arrived in sight of *Gray's Bay*, at a distance of fourteen or fifteen miles from our establishment. We had, notwithstanding, a long passage across, the river forming in this place, as I have before observed, a sort of lake, by the recession of its shores on either hand: but the wind was fair. We undertook, then, to cross and quitted the island to enter the broad, lake-like expanse just as the sun was going down, hoping to reach Astoria in a couple of hours.[76]

We were not long before we repented of our temerity: for in a short time the sky became overcast, the wind increased till it blew with violence and, meeting with the tide, caused the waves to rise prodigiously, which broke over our wretched canoe and filled it with water. We lightened it as much as we could by throwing overboard the little baggage we had left, and I set the men to baling with our remaining brass kettle. At last, after having been for three hours the sport of the raging billows and threatened every instant with being swallowed up, we had the unexpected happiness of landing in a cove on the north shore of the river. Our first care was to thank the Almighty for having delivered us from so imminent

---

[76] The escapees were put in irons. One of these men had previously planned an escape alone: Jeremy was a man of a turbulent nature who had caused some disagreements. In July, they learned that he had gathered his effects, had hidden them in the woods, and had hired four Indians to lead him a certain distance up the river. He was called to account for this, and when they went with him to the place where he had deposited its effects and exposed them to the light of day, they were not a little surprised to find there many things belonging to various other people and to the company. He was reprimanded, and was required to sign a written promise of better conduct in the future; but, as he persisted in his project, he was put in irons and all his effects were locked up. A few days afterwards, he wrote a letter of repentance; he was pardoned, and he returned to his occupations. (Stuart's Journal)

a danger. Then, when we had secured the canoe, we groped our way to the forest, where we made with branches of trees a shelter against the wind still continuing to blow with violence and kindled a great fire to warm us and dry our clothes. That did not prevent us from shivering the rest of the night, even in congratulating ourselves on the happiness of setting our foot on shore at the moment when we began quite to despair of saving ourselves at all.

The morning of the 24th brought with it a clear sky, but no abatement in the violence of the wind till toward evening, when we again embarked and arrived with our deserters at the establishment, where they never expected to see us again. Some Indians who had followed us in a canoe up to the moment when we undertook the passage across the evening before, had followed the southern shore and making the portage of the isthmus of *Tongue Point* had happily arrived at Astoria. These natives, not doubting that we were lost, so reported us to Mr. McDougal; accordingly that gentleman was equally overjoyed and astonished at beholding us safely landed, which procured, not only for us, but for the culprits, our companions, a cordial and hearty reception.

Franchere's Journal

A Voyage to the Northwest Coast of America

Chapter Six

Arrival of the Overland Party

The natives having given us to understand that
beaver was very abundant in the country wa-
tered by the Cowlitz, Mr. R. Stuart procured a
guide and set out on the 5th of December, accompanied by Messrs. Pillet[77] and McGillis[78] and
a few of the men, to ascend that river and ascertain whether or no it would be advisable to establish a trading-post on its banks. *Mr. R. Bruguier* accompanied them to follow his pursuits as a
trapper. The season at which we expected the

---

[77] Pillet is better known in the chronicles of the Northwest as B.C.
Payette. He left behind records of his own and others' adventures.
[78] Donald McGillis, a Pacific Fur Co. clerk arrived on the *Tonquin.*

return of the *Tonquin* was now past, and we began to regard as too probable the report of the Indians of *Gray's Harbor.* We still flattered ourselves, not withstanding, with the hope that perhaps that vessel had sailed for the East Indies without touching at Astoria; but this was at most a conjecture.

The 25th, Christmas Day, passed very agreeably: we treated the men on that day with the best the establishment afforded. Although that was no great affair, they seemed well satisfied; for they had been restricted during the last few months to a very meager diet, living, as one may say, on sun-dried fish. On the 27th, the schooner having returned from her second voyage up the river, we dismantled her and laid her up for the winter at the entrance of a small creek.

The weather, which had been raining almost without interruption from the beginning of October, cleared up on the evening of the 31st; and the 1st of January, 1812, brought us a clear and serene sky. We proclaimed the new year with a discharge of artillery. A small allowance of spirits was served to the men and the day passed in gayety, every one amusing himself as well as he could.

The festival over, our people resumed their ordinary occupations: while some cut timber for building and others made charcoal for the black smith, the carpenter constructed a barge and the cooper made barrels for the use of the posts we proposed to establish in the interior. On the 18th in the evening two canoes full of white men arrived at the establishment. Mr. McDougal, the resident agent, being confined to his room by sickness, the duty of receiving the strangers devolved on me. My astonishment was not slight when one of the party called me by name as he extended his hand, and I recognized Mr. Donald Mc Kenzie[79], the same who had quitted Montreal with Mr. W. P. Hunt in the month of July, 1810. He was accompanied by a Mr. Robert McClellan, a partner, Mr. John Reed, a clerk, and eight voyagers, or boatmen. After having reposed themselves a little from their fatigues, these gentle-

---

[79] Mackenzie travel west from St. Louis, Missouri with the Pacific Fur Company's overland. The groups experienced hard times in southern Idaho and divided. Mackenzie's group headed north. They canoed down the lower Snake River and the Columbia River arriving at Fort Astoria on January 18, 1812.

men recounted to us the history of their journey, of which the following is the substance.

Messrs. Hunt[80] and McKenzie, quitting Canada, proceeded by way of Mackinac and St. Louis and ascended the Missouri in the autumn of

---

[80] The Oregon Encyclopedia notes: In 1809, John Jacob Astor selected Wilson Price Hunt to be his St. Louis agent for a new enterprise—the Pacific Fur Company—and to lead an overland expedition to establish a fur post at the mouth of the Columbia River. Hunt was born at Asbury, New Jersey, in 1783. He pursued business as a young man, finding his way to St. Louis in 1804. Eager to be part of the expansive fur trade, he was motivated by information from traders and returning members of the Lewis and Clark expedition. By 1809, he became a partner, along with Canadian fur traders, in Astor's new enterprise; he received five shares. Hunt was not experienced in wilderness travel, but Astor selected him to lead the overland expedition because of his business acumen and his American citizenship. Hunt's party included sixty men, most of them Americans. Leaving St. Louis in October 1810, the men canoed some 450 miles up the Missouri River to the Aricara villages, where they headed west on horses and by foot. Hunt's leadership and diplomatic skills frequently protected his party in encounters with Indians. During the summer of 1811, the group struggled at a slow pace in the face of difficult river and mountain passages. By late September, they had reached the headwaters of the Snake River in present-day Idaho, where they descended in canoes for 200 miles through savage rapids. The party's boats were swamped and wrecked, and they lost food and supplies. Hunt decided to divide his force, each contingent to find its way to the Columbia River and descend to Astoria. Hunt and thirty men finally made it to Astoria on February 12, 1812, where they found Donald Mackenzie and ten other overlanders already there. Eventually, fifty-four members of the Hunt party arrived in safety. After five months at Astoria, Hunt sailed on Astor's supply ship, the *Beaver*, to

1810 to a place on that river called Nodaway[81] where they wintered. Here they were joined by Mr. R. McClellan,[82] by a Mr. Crooks and a Mr. Miller[83], and all having business relations with Mr. Astor.[84]

In the spring of 1811, having procured two large keelboats, they ascended the Missouri to the country of the Arikaras Indians[85] where they disposed of their boats and a great part of their luggage to a Spanish trader, by the name of

Russian Sitka in the North Pacific to promote trade between the Russian America Company and the Pacific Fur Company.

[81] Nodaway, Missouri is a former town in Andrew County, Missouri near the confluence of the Nodaway River and the Missouri River. The Lewis and Clark Expedition camped on Nodaway Island on July 8, 1804, on their travel to Oregon Country. As investors in the Astor Expedition, they recommended this location for the winter headquarters of that expedition.

[82] An overland Astorian. Alexander Ross described him as "one of the finest shots in America; nothing could escape his keen eye and steady hand; hardy, enterprising and brave as a lion."

[83] Joseph Miller was a member of the overland Astorians from October 8, 1810 in St. Louis to Fort Henry, October 9, 1811. He was a Pacific Fur Company partner and gave up his shares Fort Henry. He joined a beaver trapping party detached from the expedition; joined Stuart's eastward overland party August 20, 1812 reaching St. Louis April 30, 1813.

[84] Misters McKenzie, Crooks, Miller, McClellan, Reed, and Hunt, in company with fifty-six men, a woman, and two children traveled up the Missouri River from St. Louis . They left with eighty-two horses packing commodities, munitions, food, and animal traps. Everyone walked except the company partners and the woman, a squaw. By September the number of horses had been increased to 121. (Hunt's Journal)

[85] Indians of Arkansas

Manuel Lisa[86]. Having purchased of him and among the Indians 130 horses, they resumed their route in the beginning of August to the number of some sixty-five persons, to proceed across the mountains to the river Columbia. Wishing to avoid the Blackfoot Indians, a warlike and ferocious tribe who put to death all the strangers that fall into their hands, they directed their course southwardly until they arrived at the 40th degree of latitude. Thence they turned to the McClellan in their Upper Missouri trading enterprises.

---

[86] In April, 1811, Lisa began a final expedition of the Missouri Fur Company's first three years. The expedition became famous in its day, overtaking the barges of rival Astor on the Missouri River who had left St. Louis three week before Lisa. In September 1806, William Clark and Meriwether Lewis completed their epic journey to the Pacific Ocean, arriving back in St. Louis after more than two years in the western wilderness. Except for the difficult crossing of the Rocky Mountains, the expedition team had traveled by river. On the journey, they were overwhelmed by the abundance for beaver, otter, and other furbearing creatures they saw. The territory was ripe for fur trapping. Both Lewis and Clark recognized that sizeable fortunes could be made in fur trapping, and they were not averse to using their exclusive knowledge to gain a share of the profits. Two years after their return, Lewis and Clark helped organize the St. Louis Missouri River Fur Company. Among their partners were the experienced fur traders and businessmen Manuel Lisa, Pierre Choteau, and Auguste Choteau.

Our people, not doubting that this stream would conduct them to the Columbia, and finding it navigable, constructed some canoes to descend it. Some of the hunters (or trappers) were left near an old fort with Mr. Miller[87], who, dissatisfied with the expedition, was resolved to return to the United States. The overland party continued; but very soon finding the river obstructed with rapids and waterfalls, after having upset some of the canoes, lost one man by drowning, and also a part of their baggage, perceiving that the stream was impracticable, they resolved to abandon their canoes and proceed on foot.

---

[87] A letter of Ramsay Crooks relates some details about this eastward venture: "On June 29 or 30, 1812, a party ostensibly under the command of Robert Stuart, carrying letters and papers for Colonel Astor, set out from the recently erected post, Astoria, to return overland to the states. Stuart was accompanied by Ramsay Crooks, Robert McLellan, Benjamin Jones, Francois La Claire and Andre Vallee. Following up the Columbia and the Snake, familiar country to all of them, for they had traversed it only a few months before, they encountered just below Cauldon Linn, Joseph Miller and three others, who had been detached from the main party of Overland Astorians at Andrew Henry's abandoned post on the upper Snake River the previous October...They all proceeded together, but in a few days Miller's companions abandoned the rest of the party. Miller now undertook to pilot the remainder of their journey eastward." They reached St. Louis April 30, 1813.

The enterprise was one of great difficulty, considering the small stock of provisions they had left. Nevertheless, as there was no time to lose in deliberation, after depositing in a cache the superfluous part of their baggage they divided themselves into four companies under the command of Messrs. McKenzie, Hunt, McClellan, and Crooks, and proceeded to follow the course of the stream, which they named Mad River on account of the insurmountable difficulties it presented.

Messrs. McKenzie and McClellan took the right bank, and Messrs. Hunt and Crooks the left. They counted on arriving very quickly at the Columbia; but they followed this Mad River[88] for twenty days, finding nothing at all to eat and suffering horribly from thirst. The rocks between which the river flows being so steep and abrupt as to prevent their descending to quench their thirst (so that even their dogs died of it) they suffered the torments of Tantalus[89], with this difference that he had the water which he could not reach above his head, while our travelers had it

---

[88] Snake River.

[89] Greek God condemned to eternity with food and water just out of his reach.

beneath their feet. Several, not to die of this raging thirst, drank their own urine: all, to appease
the cravings of hunger, ate beaver skins roasted
in the evening at the campfire. They even were at
last constrained to eat their moccasins. Those on
the left or south east bank suffered, however,
less than the others, because they occasionally
fell in with Indians, utterly wild, indeed, and who
fled at their approach, carrying off their horses.

According to all appearances these savages
had never seen white men. Our travelers, when
they arrived in sight of the camp of one of these
wandering hordes, approached it with as much
precaution and with the same stratagem that
they would have used with a troop of wild beasts.
Having thus surprised them, they would fire upon the horses, some of which would fall; but they
took care to leave some trinkets on the spot to
indemnify the owners for what they had taken
from them by violence. This resource prevented
the party from perishing of hunger.

Mr. McKenzie having overtaken Mr. McClellan,
their two companies pursued the journey together. Very soon after this junction they had an

opportunity of approaching sufficiently near to Mr. Hunt, who, as I have remarked, was on the other bank, to speak to him and inform him of their distressed state. Mr. Hunt caused a canoe to be made of a horse-hide; it was not, as one may suppose, very large; but they succeeded nevertheless, by that means in conveying a little horse flesh to the people on the north bank. It was attempted, even, to pass them across, one by one (for the skiff would not hold any more); several had actually crossed to the south side when, unhappily, owing to the impetuosity of the current the canoe capsized, a man was drowned and the two parties lost all hope of being able to unite.[90]

They continued their route, therefore, each on their own side of the river. In a short time those upon the north bank came to a more considerable stream, which they followed down. They also met, very opportunely, some Indians who sold them a number of horses. They also encountered in these parts a young American who was de-

---

[90] The drowned man was Jean Baptiste Provost, a Canadian voyager. When in a starving condition, he upset his canoe in his excitement at the prospect of food.

ranged, but who sometimes recovered his reason. This young man told them, in one of his lucid intervals, that he was from Connecticut and was named Archibald Pelton; that he had come up the Missouri with Mr. Henry;[91] that all the people at the post established by that trader were massacred by the Blackfeet; that he alone had escaped, and had been wandering, for three years since, with the Snake Indians. Our people took this young man with them. Arriving at the confluence with the Columbia, of the river whose banks they were following, they perceived that it was the same which had been called Lewis River by the American captain of that name in 1805. Here, then, they exchanged their remaining horses for canoes and so arrived at the establishment, safe and sound, it is true, but in a pitiable condition to see; their clothes being nothing but fluttering rags.

---

[91] O. Ned Eddin notes: Andrew Henry of the St. Louis Missouri Fur Co. went upriver in 1810 to Montana. After being driven out of several different locations by Indians, he and his men wound up on Conant Creek (Fort Henry). In the spring of 1811, the group disbanded, each man, including Pelton, went his own direction. It is believed that Pelton had some kind of melancholia.

The narrative of these gentlemen interested us very much. They added, that since their separation from Messrs. Hunt and Crooks they had neither seen nor heard aught of them, and believed it impossible that they should arrive at the establishment before spring. They were mistaken, however, for Mr. Hunt arrived on the 15th February with thirty men, one woman, and two children[92], having left Mr. Crooks with five men among the Snakes. They might have reached Astoria almost as soon as Mr. McKenzie, but they had passed from eight to ten days in the midst of a plain, among some friendly Indians, as well to recoup their strength as to make search for two of the party who had been lost in the woods. Not finding them, they had resumed their journey and struck the banks of the Columbia a little

---

[92] These are the wife and two children Pierre Dorion, who was a Sioux half-breed; interpreter and hunter. He agreed to join the Overland Astorians in St. Louis, but backed out at the last minute unless he could take his wife and two children along, which was agreed to. He was sent to the Snake River country with the Reed party where he was killed by Indians in January, 1814. His wife, an Iowa Indian, managed to save herself and children. She later settled in the Willamette Valley where she died September 3, 1850. OHQ, XXX, 272-78.

lower down than the mouth of Lewis River, where Mr. McKenzie had come out.

The arrival of so great a number of persons would have embarrassed us had it taken place a month sooner. Happily, at this time the natives were bringing in fresh fish in abundance. Until the 30th of March we were occupied in preparing triplicates of letters and other necessary papers in order to send Mr. Astor the news of our arrival and of the reunion of the two expeditions. The letters were entrusted to Mr. John Reed, who quitted Astoria for St. Louis in company with Mr. McClellan another discontented partner who wished to disconnect himself with the association and Mr. R. Stuart, who was conveying two canoe loads of goods for his Uncle's post on the Okenakan.

Messrs. Farnham and McGillis set out at the same time, with a guide, and were instructed to proceed to the cache, where the overland travelers had hidden their goods near old Fort Henry on the Mad River.[93] I profited by this opportunity

---

[93] These caches are famous in all narratives of overland travel, whether for trade or discovery. The manner of making them is described by Captains Lewis and Clark, as follows: they choose a

to write to my family in Canada. Two days after, Messrs. McKenzie and Matthews set out, with five or six men as hunters, to make an excursion up the Willamette River.

---

dry situation, then inscribing a circle of some twenty inches diameter, remove the sod as gently and carefully as possible. The hole is then sunk a foot deep or more, perpendicularly, then it is worked gradually wider as it descends, till it becomes six or seven feet deep, and shaped like a kettle, or the lower part of a large still. As the earth is dug out, it is handed up in a vessel, and carefully laid on a skin or a clothe, in which it is carried away and usually thrown into the river, if there is one, or concealed as to leave no trace of it. A floor of three or four inches thick of dried sticks on which is thrown hay or a hide which is perfectly dry. The goods, after being aired and dried, are laid down, and preserved from contact with the walls by another layer of dried sticks till all is stowed away. When the hole is nearly full, a hide is laid on top, and the earth is then thrown upon this, and beaten down, until, with the addition of the first sod removed, the hole is on a level with the ground, and there remains not the slightest appearance of an excavation. The first shower effaces every sign of what had been done, and such a cache is safe for years. (Huntington)

Franchere's Journal

A Voyage to the Northwest Coast of America

Chapter Seven
Trading and Exploring Activities

From the departure of the last outfit under Mr.
McKenzie nothing remarkable took place at Astoria till the 9th of May. On that day we de-
scried, to our great surprise and great joy, a sail
in the offing opposite the mouth of the river.
Forthwith Mr. McDougal was dispatched in a
boat to the cape to make signals.[94] On the morning of the 10th, 1812, the weather being fine and
the sea smooth, the boat pushed out and arrived
safely alongside. Soon after, the wind springing

---

[94] Mr. McDougall and several others climbed Cape Disappointment and set some trees on fire to serve as an impromptu light
house for the *Beaver* for making an entrance into the Columbia
River. Captain Sowles thought the signal might be treachery and
anchored off shore until the next day when an Indian canoe and
Comcomly with six Indians and a barge with McDougall and some
Canadians arrived alongside the *Beaver*.

up, the vessel made sail and entered the river, where she dropped anchor in *Baker Bay*, at about 2 P. M. Toward evening a boat came to the Fort, with the following passengers: Messrs. John Clarke[95] of Canada (a wintering partner), Alfred Seton[96], George Ehnainger, a nephew of Mr. Astor (clerks), and two men. We learned from these gentlemen that the vessel was the *Beaver*, Captain Cornelius Sowles[97], and was consigned to us; that she left New York on the 10th of October and had touched, in the passage, at Massa Fuero and the Sandwich Isles. Mr. Clarke handed me letters from my father and from several of my friends: I thus learned that death had deprived me of a beloved sister.

---

[95] Clarke appeared to be a nephew of Astor. He commanded a second expedition to Fort Astoria in 1811 and was present when the Fort was surrendered to the North West Company in 1812.

[96] Seton grew up in privileged New York Mercantile family whose circumstances had been reduced by economic difficulties. He had just finished his second year at Columbia University when he joined Astor's Pacific Fur Company under a five year contract, hoping to return to New York a wealthy man.

[97] Bancroft notes: The only vessel known to have touched the Northwest coast in 1812 was the *Beaver*, commanded by Captain Cornelius Sowles. She brought from New York another detachment of Astor's fur company , and entered the Columbia River on May 10. She left the river in August and proceeded on a trading tour up the coast. The intension was to return to Astoria, but the vessel proceeded from Sitka to the Sandwich Islands and China.

On the morning of the 9th we were strangely surprised by the return of Messrs. D. Stuart, R. Stuart, R. McClellan, Crooks, Reed, and Farnham[98]. This return, as sudden as unlooked for, was owing to an unfortunate adventure which befell the party, in ascending the river. When they reached the Falls, where the portage is very long, some natives came with their horses to offer their aid in transporting the goods. Mr. R. Stuart, not distrusting them, confided to their care some bales of merchandise which they packed on their horses: but in making the transit they darted up a narrow path among the rocks and fled at full gallop toward the prairie, without its being possible to overtake them. Mr. Stuart

---

[98] Farnham joined Astor's Pacific Fur Company as a clerk in 1810 and arrived at the mouth of the Columbia River on the *Tonquin*. He helped build the fort in the spring of 1811 and was later sent to trade with the Salish (Flathead) tribe near present-day Thompson Falls, Montana. When control of the fort passed to the British, Farnham and several other stranded Americans left on the brig *Pedler* with Wilson P. Hunt, who had been in charge of the fort. Farnham served as third officer under Captain Northrop. At the Russian settlement in present-day Sitka, Alaska, Farnham joined the crew of the *Forester* under Captain William Pigot and traveled to Kamchatka, Russia. The captain sent him overland to St. Petersburg with the proceeds of the sale of the ship's cargo of furs. He then traveled back to New York through Copenhagen. (James Kelly)

had several shots fired over their heads to frighten them but it had no other effect than to increase their speed.

Meanwhile our own people continued the transportation of the rest of the goods and of the canoes[99]; but as there was a great number of natives about, whom the success and impunity of those thieves had emboldened, Mr. Stuart thought it prudent to keep watch over the goods at the upper end of the portage while Messrs. McLellan and Reed made the rearguard. The last named gentleman, who carried strapped to his shoulders a tin box containing the letters and dispatches for New York with which he was charged, happened to be at some distance from

---

[99] During the ten days following the anchoring of the *Beaver* in Baker's Bay on the north side of the Columbia River, small boats ferried the $30,000 worth of cargo from the ship to the fort. The first order of business was to unload the livestock: goats, birds and 50 hogs acquired in Hawaii. The post supplies included carpentry tools; a blacksmith's forge and bellow; muskets and bayonets; rice, molasses and coffee; a military drum and two fifes; a crate of dishes with "fancy bowls" and an enameled tea pot; two boxes of sigars (cigars); casks of rum, gin, Madeira wine, ale and whiskey; 500 pounds of soap; seeds of onions, turnips, carrots, radishes, muskmelon, and four types of cabbages. The new assortment of trade goods included several hogsheads of tobacco; bales of cotton and woolen clothe; 500 fish hooks; 15 dozen pails; 800 pounds of beads; 109 men's felt hats; and eight bales of handkerchiefs. (Historylink.org)

the former, and the Indians thought it a favorable opportunity to attack him and carry off his box, the brightness of which no doubt had tepted their cupidity. They threw themselves upon him so suddenly that he had no time to place himself on the defensive. After a short resistance he received a blow on the head from a war club which felled him to the ground, and the Indians seized upon their booty. Mr. McLellan perceiving what was done, fired his carbine at one of the robbers and made him bite the dust; the rest took to flight, but carried off the box notwithstanding. Mr. McLellan immediately ran up to Mr. Reed; but finding the latter motionless and bathed in blood, he hastened to rejoin Mr. Stuart, urging him to get away from these robbers and murderers. But Mr. Stuart being a self-possessed and fearless man, would not proceed without ascertaining if Mr. Reed were really dead, or, if he were, without carrying off his body; and notwithstanding the remonstrance's of Mr. McLellan, taking his way back to the spot where the latter had left his companion, had not gone two hundred paces when he met him coming toward them, holding his bleeding head with both hands.

The object of Mr. Reed's journey being defeated by the loss of his papers, he repaired with the other gentlemen to Mr. David Stuart's trading post at Okanakan, whence they had all set out in the beginning of May to return to Astoria.[100]

Coming down the river, they fell in with Mr. R. Crooks[101] and a man named John Day[102]. It was

---

[100] The first interior fort of the Pacific Company was placed on the east bank of the Okanakan River a few miles above its mouth. It was a stopping place for the Overland brigade, and in due time became the chief station for the deposit of furs from the New Caledonian district.(Bancroft)

[101] Crooks was born in Greenock, Scotland, January 28, 1786, and came in early life to what is now Wisconsin. Previous to joining interests with Astor, he and McLellan had journeyed far towards the head waters of the Missouri. At Mackinac Island and on his adventurous trips he was a great friend and confidant of the Indians. Black Hawk said he was "the best pale-face friend the red man ever had." Crooks not only made the 3,500 mile trip out of Astoria, but was lost from the main party and spent the entire winter among hostile Indians in the Rocky Mountains. On reaching Astoria, he was the first to accompany young Robert Stuart on the memorial journey to St. Louis. In 1834 he settled in New York City and prospered in business, dying there on June 6, 1859.

[102] Thwaites notes: John Day was a Virginian who hunted some time on the Missouri, and had been in Crooks employ. He joined the overland Astoria at its winter quarters at Nodaway. Upon the outward journey Day and Crook were left behind, being robbed and stripped by the Indians on the Columbia. They were rescued and carried to Astoria by John Stuart's party. Day started to return with the overland party in 1813, but was taken violently

88

observed in the preceding chapter that Mr. Crooks remained with five men among some Indians who were there termed friendly: but this gentleman and his companion were the only members of that party who ever reached the establishment: and they, too, arrived in a most pitiable condition, the savages having stripped them of everything, leaving them but some bits of deerskin to cover their nakedness.

On the 12th the schooner, which had been sent down the river to the *Beaver*'s anchorage, returned with a cargo (being the stores intended for Astoria), and the following passengers: to wit, Messrs. B. Clapp, J. C. Halsey[103], C. A. Nichols,[104] and R. Cox[105], clerks; five Canadians,

---

insane, and attempted his own life. He was sent back to Astoria. There is evidence that he joined the North West Company and lived until 1819.

[103] J.C. Halsey, a clerk of the Pacific Fur Company, arrived on the *Beaver* May 12, 1812. He was one of five clerks who had so arrived under partner John Clarke. He was sent from Astoria Nov. 12, 1812, with William Wallace and 14 men to establish a post on the Willamette River and returned the following May. He finally left Fort George on the Brig. *Pedlar*, April 2, 1814, and was landed in Sitka when the Brig went on.

[104] A Pacific Fur Company employee who arrived at Astoria on the *Beaver*.

[105] Ross Cox, who bore the soubriquet "Little Irishman," entered North West service and remained upon Columbian waters for six

seven Americans (all mechanics), and a dozen Sandwich Islanders for the service of the establishment. The captain of the *Beaver* sounded the channel diligently for several days; but finding it scarcely deep enough for so large a vessel, he was unwilling to bring her up to Astoria. It was necessary, in consequence, to use the schooner as a lighter in discharging the ship, and this tedious operation occupied us during the balance of this month and a part of June.

Captain Sowles and Mr. Clarke confirmed the report of the destruction of the *Tonquin*; they had learned it at Owyhee by means of a letter which a certain Captain Ebbetts, in the employ of Mr. Astor, had left there. It was nevertheless resolved that Mr. Hunt should embark upon the *Beaver* to carry out the plan of an exact commercial survey of the coast which Mr. McKay had been sent to accomplish, and in particular to visit for that purpose the Russian establishment at Chitka [Sitka] Sound.

The necessary papers having been prepared anew, and being now ready to expedite, were

---

years ascending from its mouth nine times. In 1831 he published an entertaining narrative entitled, *Adventures upon the Columbia River.*

confided to Mr. R. Stuart, who was to cross the continent in company with Messrs. Crooks and R. McClellan, partners dissatisfied with the enterprise, and who had made up their minds to return to the United States. Mr. Clarke, accompanied by Messrs. Pillet, Donald, McLennan, Farnham[106], and Cox, was fitted out at the same time with a considerable assortment of merchandise to form a new establishment on the *Spokan* or *Clarke's River.* Mr. McKenzie, with Mr. Seton, was destined for the borders of *Lewis River.* while Mr. David Stuart, reinforced by Messrs. Matthews and McGillis, was to explore the region lying north of his post at Okenakan. All these outfits being ready, with the canoes, boatmen, and hunters, the flotilla quitted Astoria on the 30th of June in the afternoon, having on board sixty-two persons.

During the whole month of July the natives (seeing us weakened, no doubt, by these outfits),

---

[106] Russell Farnham of Massachusetts, Pacific Fur Company clerk had came to Astoria on the *Tonquin.* March 30, 1812 he left with a party in search of a cache left in Idaho by the overland Astorians. In 1813 he spent a considerable time at the Spokane House. Finally in 1814 he left Fort George aboard the *Pedlar* for Sitka, Kamchatka, etc., and went around the world by land and sea before landing in New York. (Henry and Thompson)

manifested their hostile intentions so openly that we were obliged to be constantly on our guard. We constructed covered ways inside our palisades and raised our bastions or towers another story. The alarm became so serious toward the latter end of the month that we doubled our sentries day and night, and never allowed more than two or three Indians at a time within our gates.

The *Beaver* was ready to depart on her coasting voyage at the end of June, and on the 1st of July Mr. Hunt went on board: but westerly winds prevailing all that month, it was not till the 4th of August that she was able to get out of the river; being due again by the end of October to leave her surplus goods and take in our furs for market.

The months of August and September were employed in finishing a house forty-five feet by thirty, shingled and perfectly tight, as a hospital for the sick and lodging house for the mechanics.

Experience having taught us that from the beginning of October to the end of January provisions were brought in by the natives in very small quantity, it was thought expedient that I should proceed in the schooner, accompanied by Mr. Clapp, on a trading voyage up the river to secure a cargo of dried fish. We left Astoria on the 1st of October with a small assortment of merchandise. The trip was highly successful: we found the game very abundant, killed a great quantity of swans, ducks, foxes, etc., and returned to Astoria on the 20th with a part of our venison, wild fowl, and bear meat besides seven hundred and fifty smoked salmon, a quantity of the Wapato root[107] (so called by the natives), which is found a good substitute for potatoes, and four hundred and fifty skins of beaver and other animals of the furry tribe.

The encouragement derived from this excursion induced us to try a second, and I set off this

---

[107] The Wapato root came to the attention of the Lewis and Clark expedition on October 22, 1805 at the mouth of the Deschutes River. Meriwether Lewis temporarily dropped behind the rest of the party "to examine a root which the native had been digging great quantities in the bottom" of the river. The leaf stems spring from the plant, celery like. Below in the muck, are rhizomes that produce small starchy tubers at their tips, in the way potatoes do. This play still grows, in a dozen different species and varieties in all lower 48 states, except Nevada, and in southern Canada. The Captains named today's Sauvie Island, in the Columbia River off Multnomah Country Oregon, "Wappetoe Island."

time alone, that is, with a crew of five men only and an Indian boy, son of the old chief Comcomly. This second voyage proved anything but agreeable. We experienced continual rains and the game was much less abundant, while the natives had mostly left the river for their wintering grounds. I succeeded, nevertheless, in exchanging my goods for furs and dried fish and a small supply of dried venison: and returned on the 15th of November to Astoria, where want of fresh provisions began to be severely felt, so that several of the men were attacked with scurvy.

Messrs. Halsey and Wallace having been sent on the 23d with fourteen men to establish a trading post on the Willamette[108] and Mr. McDougal being confined to his room by sickness, Mr. Clapp and I were left with the entire charge of the post at Astoria, and were each other's only resource for society. Happily Mr. Clapp was a man of amiable character, of a gay, lively humor and agreeable conversation. In the intervals of our daily duties we amused ourselves with music

---

[108] The camp of Halsey and Wallace was located upon a small prairie situated just north of where the Oregon State Mute School was established which was called Wallace's Prairie in the 1840 and was later known as the Bush farm.

and reading, having some instruments and a nice library.[109] Otherwise we should have passed our time in a state of insufferable ennui at this rainy season, in the midst of the deep mud which surrounded us and which interdicted the pleasure of a promenade outside the buildings.

---

[109] On the invoice of merchandise shipped by John Astor on board *the Beaver* and consigned to the establishment at Astoria is a long list of books that, apparently, became the "library." It included such works as Carr's *Scotland*, Pindar's *Works*, Burn's *Poems* (2 vols.), and a *History of Chile*.

A Voyage to the Northwest Coast of America

Chapter Eight
War and Confusion

The months of October, November, and December passed away without any news of the *Beaver* [110] and we began to fear that there had happened to her, as to the *Tonquin,* some disastrous accident. It will be seen in the following chapter why this vessel did not return to Astoria in the autumn of 1812.

On the 15th of January Mr. McKenzie arrived from the interior, having abandoned his trading establishment, after securing his stock of goods in a cache. Before his departure he had paid a

---

[110] The Beaver arrived at St. Paul's Island on the 31st of October; by which time, according to arrangement, he ought to have been back at Astoria but Hunt made an agreement with Baranov to pick up seal furs in St. Paul. One night, while Mr. Hunt was on shore, with some others of the crew, there arose a terrible gale. When the day broke, the ship was not to be seen. At length, on the 13th of November, the *Beaver* made her appearance; much the worse for the storm than she had sustained in those hyperborean seas. The ship and the sails were in such poor condition that Hunt felt that returning to the Columbia River at this time of year was out of the question. Accordingly the *Beaver* was sailed to Canton where the furs were sold and the ship repaired before heading for the Sandwich Islands and then on to Astoria aboard the *Pedlar.*

visit to Mr. Clarke on the *Spokan*, and while there had learned the news, which he came to announce to us, that hostilities had actually commenced between Great Britain and the United States. The news had been brought by some gentlemen of the North West Company,[111] who handed to them a copy of the Proclamation of the President to that effect.

When we learned this news all of us at Astoria who were British subjects and Canadians wished ourselves in Canada; but we could not entertain even the thought of transporting ourselves thither, at least immediately; we were separated from our country by an immense space, and the difficulties of the journey at this season were insuperable: besides, Mr. Astor's interests had to be consulted first. We held, therefore, a sort of

---

[111] The North West Company, founded in 1783, was a Canadian fur trading company, once the chief rival of the Hudson's Bay Company that was chartered by English government. The North West company enjoyed rapid growth. Its operations were originally centered in the Lake Superior region and the valleys of the Red, Assiniboine and Saskatchewan rivers but later spread north and west to the shores of the Arctic and Pacific Oceans. They even constructed posts in what is now Washington and Idaho. Later, open conflict broke out between these two companies. Under pressure from the British government, the two companies were merged in 1821.

council of war, to which the clerks of the factory were invited proforma[112], as they had no voice in the deliberations. Having maturely weighed our situation; after having seriously considered that being almost to a man British subjects we were trading, notwithstanding, under the American flag: and foreseeing the improbability, or rather, to cut the matter short, the impossibility that Mr. Astor could send us further supplies or reinforcements while the war lasted, as most of the ports of the United States would inevitably be blockaded by the British; we concluded to abandon the establishment in the ensuing spring or, at latest, in the beginning of the summer. We did not communicate these resolutions to the men lest they should in consequence abandon their labor: but we discontinued from that moment our trade with the natives, except for provisions; as well because we had no longer a large stock of goods on hand, as for the reason that we had already more furs than we could carry away overland.

---

[112] The clerks were not allowed to vote.

So long as we expected the return of the vessel we had served out to the people a regular supply of bread: we found ourselves, in consequence, compelled to reduce the ration of each man to four ounces of flour and half a pound of dried fish per diem: and even to send a portion of the hands to pass the rest of the winter with Messrs. Wallace and Halsey on the Willamette, where game was plentiful.

Meanwhile, the sturgeon having begun to enter the river, I left on the 12th of February to fish for them; and on the 15th sent the first boat-load to the establishment; which proved a very timely succor to the men, who for several days had broken off work from want of sufficient food. I formed a camp near Oak Point where I continued to dispatch canoe after canoe of fine fresh fish to Astoria, and Mr. McDougall sent to me thither all the men who were sick of scurvy, for the re-establishment of their health.

On the 20th of March Messrs. Reed[113] and Seton[114], who had led a part of our men to the

---

[113] John Reed, a clerk of Irish birth; the only clerk with the overland expedition, more mature and more active than the other clerks engaged in this enterprise; joined expedition at Mackinac

post on the Willamette to subsist them, returned to Astoria with a supply of dried venison. These gentlemen spoke to us in glowing terms of the country of the Willamette as charming, and abounding in beaver, elk, and deer; and informed us that Messrs. Wallace and Halsey had constructed a dwelling and trading house on a great prairie, about one hundred and fifty miles from the confluence of that river with the Columbia. Mr. McKenzie and his party quitted us again on the 31st to make known the resolutions recently adopted at Astoria to the gentlemen who were wintering in the interior.

On the 9th of April two birch-bark canoes, bearing the British flag, arrived at the factory. They were commanded by Messrs. *J. G. McTa-*

---

with McClellan, McKenzie and eight voyagers arriving in Astoria January 18, 1812. Left Astoria March 1812, but was attacked by Indians and forced to return; sent with a party to the Snake River region in the summer of 1813; killed there in January, 1814.

[114] Alfred Seton was a clerk of Pacific Fur Company who arrived on the *Beaver* and was stationed at the post in Champoeg by 1814. C.C. Dodds in *Men of Champoeg* noted: Etienne Lucier with William Cannon and Joseph Gervais (all overland Astorians) were the earliest arrivals among the settlers, coming with the Wilson Hunt party in 1812 to establish John Jacob Astor's trading post on the Columbia. When this venture was taken over by the English, Lucier worked as trapper under the British company.

point of land under the guns of the fort and formed their camp. We invited these gentlemen to our quarters and learned from them the object of their visit. They had come to await the arrival of the ship *Isaac Todd*[116], dispatched from Canada by *Joseph Larocque* who had an elder brother, *Frangois,* who figures in the narratives of the *Lewis and Clark expedition.*[117] In the winter of 1804-1805, as a clerk employed by the *North West Company*[118] he led a party from *Fort Assini-*

---

[116] The *Isaac Todd* arrived at Astoria in 1814. She had transferred part of her cargo and orders, to annihilate any American settlement to the Raccoon. By the time the *Raccoon* arrived at Astoria in November, 1813, it was no longer an American settlement.

[117] On November 11, 1804, Larocque and six companions, with nine horses. five of which were loaded with trade goods, set out for the Mandan settlements at the mouth of the Knife River on the Missouri. The trade goods included tools such as axes, knives, awls, flints and steels for fire-starting, and a quantity of powder and ball. There was tobacco, too, and personal items such as combs and beads. Fourteen days later, on November 24, the party arrived at the middle Minitari (Hidatsa) village, known as Metaharta, where Larocque was to look up an interpreter named Toussaint Charbonneau—the very same Charbonneau who would be hired by Lewis and Clark the following March 18. Charbonneau was not at home. The next day, however, on the road to the nearby Mandan villages, young Larocque chanced to meet Charbonneau, the free trader René Jusseaume, and Meriwether Lewis. For about a quarter of an hour he chatted with Lewis, who invited him to Fort Mandan, "& appeared very friendly." (Discovering Lewis and Clark)

[118] Several principal merchants of Montreal entered into a partnership in the winter of 1783, which was augmented by amalgamation with a rival company in 1787. Thus was created the famous "Northwest Company," which for a time held a lordly sway over the wintry lakes and boundless forests of the Canadas, almost equal to that of the East India Company

boine[119] to the *Mandans* where Lewis and Clark were wintering, and from June to October, 1805 he was engaged upon a tour to the Rocky Mountains the *North West Company* in October, 1811 with furs, and from England in March, 1812 with a cargo of suitable merchandise for the Indian trade. They had orders to wait at the mouth of the Columbia till the month of July, and then to return, if the vessel did not make her appearance

over the voluptuous climes and magnificent realms of the Orient. The company consisted of twenty-three shareholders, or partners, but held in its employ about two thousand persons as clerks, guides, interpreters, and "voyageurs," or boatmen. These were distributed at various trading posts, established far and wide on the interior lakes and rivers, at immense distances from each other, and in the heart of trackless countries and savage tribes. Several of the partners resided in Montreal and Quebec, to manage the main concerns of the company. These were called agents, and were personages of great weight and importance; the other partners took their stations at the interior posts, where they remained throughout the winter, to superintend the intercourse with the various tribes of Indians. They were thence called wintering partners. (Irwin, *Astoria*)

[119] Fort Assiniboine (Brandon House) was a Hudson's Bay Company post or posts from 1793 to 1824. It was located at several places on the Assiniboine River between Brandon, Manitoba and the mouth of the Souris River about 21 miles southeast of Brandon. Because of its location near the Souris River it was a center for trade with the Mandans in North Dakota. It was moved four times and there were related forts near-by, so its history is necessarily complex. In 1797 David Thompson passed through on his way to determine the latitude and longitude of the Mandan villages. In 1804, when the NWC absorbed the XY Company, Fort Assiniboine was moved across the river to the site of Fort La Souris#1. In 1806 Alexander Henry passed through. The man in charge was Francois-Antoine Larocque who later reached the Yellowstone River. In 1807 the fort was torn down and its parts rafted downstream to Fort des Epinettes. (Wikipedia)

by that time. They also informed us that the natives near *Lewis River* had shown them fowling-pieces, gun-flints, lead, and powder; and that they had communicated this news to Mr. McKenzie, presuming that the Indians had discovered and plundered his cache; which turned afterward to be the case.

The month of May was occupied in preparations for our departure from the Columbia. On the 25th Messrs. Wallace and Halsey[120] returned from their winter quarters with seventeen packs of furs and thirty-two bales of dried venison. The last article was received with a great deal of pleasure, as it would infallibly be needed for the journey we were about to undertake. Messrs. Clarke, D. Stuart, and McKenzie also arrived in the beginning of June with one hundred and forty packs of furs, the fruit of two years' trade at the post on the Okenakane, and one year on the Spokane rivers.

---

[120] Ruby and Brown note: Astorian Clerks William Wallace and John Halsey established a post up the Willamette River near present day Salem, Oregon in late 1812 or early 1813. There they took furs mainly from free hunters rather than Indians of the area who were probably unfamiliar with fur-gathering activities.

The wintering partners (that is to say, Messrs. Clarke and David Stuart) dissenting from the proposal to abandon the country as soon as we intended, the thing being (as they observed) impracticable from the want of provisions for the journey and horses to transport the goods, the project was deferred, as to its execution, till the following April. So these gentlemen, having taken a new lot of merchandise, set out again for their trading posts on the 7th of July. But Mr. McKenzie, whose goods had been pillaged by the natives (it will be remembered), remained at Astoria, and was occupied with the care of collecting as great a quantity as possible of dried salmon from the Indians. He made seven or eight voyages up the river for that purpose while we at the Fort were busy in baling the beaver skins and other furs in suitable packs for horses to carry. Mr. Reed, in the meantime, was sent on to the mountain-passes where Mr. Miller had been left with the trappers, to winter there and to procure as many horses as he could from the natives for our use on the contemplated journey.

He was furnished for this expedition with three

Canadians and a half-breed hunter named Dai-on, the latter accompanied by his wife and two children. who came from Missouri with Hunt.

Our object being to provide ourselves, before quitting the country, with the food and horses necessary for the journey; in order to avoid all opposition on the part of the North West Company, we entered into an arrangement with Mr. McTavish. This gentleman having represented to us that he was destitute of the necessary goods to procure wherewith to subsist his party on their way homeward, we supplied him from our warehouse, payment to be made us in the ensuing spring either in furs or in bills of exchange on their house in Canada.

At this juncture "One of our young men, Rosenberg Cox[121], preferred to engage in the service of the (North West) Company rather than cross the Continent with us."

---

[121] Ross Cox, fur trader and author, was born in Dublin in 1793 and died there sixty years later. Not much is known about his childhood or arrival in America. At the age of 18 he signed on as a clerk with Pacific Fur Company for $100 per year and sailed to Astoria aboard the *Beaver.* At the end of June, 1812, Cox left Astoria with Clark to set up a post on the Spokane River near that of the North West Company. Cox would later join that Company.

Franchere's Journal

A Voyage to the Northwest Coast of America

Chapter Nine

The Fate of the *Tonquin*

On the 4th of August, contrary to all expectation we saw a sail at the mouth of the river. One of our gentlemen immediately got into the barge to ascertain her nationality and object: but before he had fairly crossed the river we saw her pass the bar and direct her course toward Astoria, as if she were commanded by a captain to whom the intricacies of the channel were familiar. I had stayed at the Fort with Mr. *Clapp*[122] and four

---

[122] Neilson Barry notes: Benjamin Clapp sailed on the *Beaver* from New York Oct. 10, 1811 arriving at Astoria May 12, 1812 and worked with Franchere as a clerk. He accompanied Franchere on a voyage on the *Dolly* and shortly thereafter married a Chinook woman. In October of 1813 Clapp sailed on the *Albatross* with Mr. Hunt to Marquesas Island where there was an American ship-of-war with several and British whalers it had

men. As soon as we had recognized the American flag, not doubting any longer that it was a ship destined for the factory we saluted her with three guns. She came to anchor over against the fort, but on the opposite side of the river, and returned our salute. In a short time after we saw, or rather we heard, the oars of a boat (for it was already night) that came toward us. We expected her approach with impatience, to know who the stranger was and what news she brought us. Soon we were relieved from our uncertainty by the appearance of Mr. Hunt, who informed us that the ship was called the *Albatross* and was commanded by Captain Smith.

It will be remembered that Mr. Hunt had sailed from Astoria on board the *Beaver* on the 4th of August of the preceding year, and should have returned with that vessel in the month of October of the same year. We testified to him our surprise that he had not returned at the time ap-

captured. Clapp joined the U.S. Navy as a midshipman. Six months later he was taken prisoner aboard the British ship *Charon*. In December, 1814 he was released in Reo de Janeiro. Records indicate that he requested a leave of absence from the Navy in December, 1815, which was granted. A pencil line was drawn through his name with the word "Resigned" written next to it. Clapp eventually made his way back to New York.

pointed, and expressed the fears which we entertained in regard to his fate, as well as that of the *Beaver* itself: and in reply he explained to us the reasons why neither he nor Captain Sowles had been able to fulfill the promise which they had made us.

After having got clear of the river Columbia, they had scudded to the north, and had repaired to the Russian post of Sitka, where they had exchanged a part of their goods for furs. They had made with the governor of that establishment, Baranov by name, arrangements to supply him regularly with all the goods of which he had need, and to send him every year a vessel for that purpose, as well as for the transportation of his surplus furs to the East Indies.

These operations had consumed a great deal of time; the season was already far advanced; ice was forming around them, and it was not without having incurred considerable dangers that they succeeded in making their way out of those latitudes. Having extricated themselves from the frozen seas of the north, but in a shattered condition, they deemed it more prudent to run for the Sandwich Isles, where they arrived after enduring a succession of severe gales. Here Mr. Hunt disembarked, with the men who had accompanied him, and who did not form a part of the ship's crew; and the vessel, after undergoing the necessary repairs, set sail for Canton.

Mr. Hunt had then passed nearly six months at the Sandwich Islands, expecting the annual ship from New York and never imagining that war had been declared. But at last, weary of waiting so long to no purpose, he had bought a small schooner of one of the chiefs of the isle of Owahou, and was engaged in getting her ready to sail for the mouth of the Columbia when four sails hove in sight and presently came to anchor in Whytiti Bay. He immediately went on board of one of them and learned that they came from the Indies, whence they had sailed precipitately to avoid the English cruisers. He also learned from the captain of the vessel he boarded that the *Beaver* had arrived in Canton some days before the news of the declaration of war. This Captain Smith, moreover, had on board some cases of nankeens and other goods shipped by Mr. Astor's agent at Canton for us. Mr. Hunt then chartered the *Albatross* to take him with his people and the goods to the Columbia. That gentleman had not been idle during the time that he sojourned at Owahou: he brought us 35 barrels of salt pork or beef, nine tierces of rice, a great quantity of dried taro, and a good supply of salt.

As I knew the channel of the river I went on board the *Albatross* and piloted her to the old anchorage of the *Tonquin* under the guns of the Fort, in order to facilitate the landing of the goods.

Captain Smith[123] informed us that in 1810, a year before the founding of our establishment, he had entered the river in the same vessel and ascended it in boats as far as *Oak Point*; and that he had attempted to form an establishment there; but the spot which he chose for building, and on which he had even commenced fencing for a garden, being overflowed in the summer

---

[123] William Smith, born in Virginia in 1768, migrated to Boston and in 1790 began a life upon the ocean, in which he made eight voyage around the world, on one of which he was absent eight years. Once he was ship and twice taken prisoner - by the Indians on the Northwest coast and by the Spanish in California. He was first mate on the *Albatross* when she made her first voyage up the Columbia River in 1810, Nathan Winship being in charge. He later became captain of the vessel.

freshet, he had been forced to abandon his pro-ject and re-embark. We had seen, in fact, at *Oak Point* some traces of this projected establish-ment. The bold manner in which this Captain had entered the river was now accounted for.

Captain Smith had chartered his vessel to a Frenchman named *Demestre*, who was then a passenger on board of her, to go and take a cargo of sandalwood at the Marquesas, where that gen-tleman had left some men to collect it the year before. He could not, therefore, comply with the request we made him to remain during the sum-mer with us in order to transport our goods and people, as soon as they could be got together, to the *Sandwich Islands*.

Mr. Hunt was surprised beyond measure when we informed him of the resolution we had taken of abandoning the country: he blamed us se-verely for having acted with so much precipita-tion, pointing out that the success of the late coasting voyage and the arrangements we had made with the *Russians* promised a most advan-tageous trade, which it was a thousand pities to sacrifice and lose the fruits of the hardships he had endured and the dangers he had braved, at one fell swoop, by this rash measure.

Nevertheless, seeing the partners were determined to abide by their first resolution, and not being able, by himself alone, to fulfill his engagements to *Governor Baranov*,[124] he consented to embark once more, in order to seek a vessel to transport our heavy goods and such of us as wished to return by sea. He sailed, in fact, on the *Albatross* at the end of the month.

My friend *Clapp* embarked with him: they were, in the first instance, to run down the coast of California, in the hope of meeting there some of

---

[124] Alexander Baranof was a Russian native, born in 1747. He grew to become a successful merchant in Irkutsk, Siberia, but he was lured to Alaska by the region's rapidly expanding fur trading industry. Baranov became quite successful in his Alaskan ventures also. He established and managed trading posts throughout the Kodiak Island region. He set up trading posts in St. Paul's Harbor, Cook Inlet, and Prince William Sound, and was instrumental in establishing colonies throughout the region. In 1799 he became chief manager for the profitable and influential Russian American Company, and over saw all of Alaska, including the Aleutian and Kurile Islands. Activity in the region flourished as trading in sea otters and seals boomed. In addition to establishing trading centers and presiding over vast expanses of territory, Baranov is credited with organizing native Alaskan hunters to expand their range and include the coasts of California. Baranov also advocated more educational opportunities for native Alaskans. Under his leadership, schools were created and frontier communities became less isolated.

the American vessels which frequently visit that coast to obtain provisions from the Spaniards.

Some days after the departure of *Mr. Hunt*, the old one-eyed chief *Comcomly* came to tell us that an Indian[125] of *Gray's Harbor*, who had sailed on the *Tonquin* in 1811, and who was the only soul that had escaped the massacre of the crew of that unfortunate vessel, had returned to his tribe. As the distance from the river Columbia to *Gray's Harbor* was not great, we sent for this native. At first he made considerable difficulty about following our people, but was finally persuaded. He arrived at Astoria and related to us the circumstances of that sad catastrophe nearly as follows: "After I had embarked on the Tonquin," said he, "that vessel sailed for Nootka."

Having arrived opposite a large village called Newitte[126], we dropped anchor. The natives hav-

---

[125] He is identified as George Ramsey, the son of a shipwrecked British sailor and a Chehalis woman, who went along as a guide and interpreter. He is frequently referred to as Lamasee (Seton).

[126] or Clatilseaquilla. Ruby and Brown note: Locations given for the destruction of the *Tonquin* have varied. It seems rather conclusive from evidence obtained from a Vancouver Island native by Augustine J. Brabant, a Roman Catholic missionary at Hesquiot on the west coast of Vancouver Island, that the site was near the tree and brushwood-covered Lennard Island, called *Eitsape* by

ing invited Mr. McKay to land, he did so and was received in the most cordial manner: they even kept him several days at their village and made him lie every night on a couch of sea-otter skins. Meanwhile, the Captain was engaged in trading with such of the natives as resorted to his ship: but having had a difficulty with one of the principal chiefs in regard to the price of certain goods, he ended by putting the latter out of the ship and in the act of so repelling him struck him on the face with the roll of furs which he had brought to trade. This act was regarded by that chief and his followers as the most grievous insult, and they resolved to take vengeance for it. To arrive more surely at their purpose they dissembled their resentment and came, as usual, on board the ship. One day, very early in the morning, a large pirogue containing about a score of natives came alongside: every man had in his hand a packet of furs, and held it over his head as a sign that they came to trade. The watch let them come on deck. A little after, ar-

---

the natives and near a long barren rocky village Island in Templar Channel leading into Clayoquot Sound.

rived a second pirogue, carrying about as many men as the other. The sailors believed that these also came to exchange their furs and allowed them to mount the ship's side like the first. Very soon, the pirogues thus succeeding one another, the crew saw themselves surrounded by a multitude of savages, who came upon the deck from all sides. Becoming alarmed at the appearance of things, they went to apprise the Captain and Mr, McKay, who hastened to the poop. I was with them," said the narrator, "and fearing, from the great multitude of Indians whom I saw already on the deck and from the movements of those on shore, who were hurrying to embark in their canoes to approach the vessel, and from the women being left in charge of the canoes of those who had arrived, that some evil design was on foot, I communicated my suspicions to Mr. McKay, who himself spoke to the Captain. The latter affected an air of security and said that with the firearms on board, there was no reason to fear even a greater number of Indians. Meanwhile, these gentlemen had come on deck unarmed, without even their side arms.

The trade, nevertheless, did not advance; the Indians offered less than was asked, and pressing with their furs close to the Captain, Mr. McKay, and Mr. Lewis, repeated the word Makoke! Makoke! 'Trade! Trade!' I urged the gentlemen to put to sea, and the Captain, at last, seeing the number of Indians increase every moment, allowed himself to be persuaded: he ordered a part of the crew to raise the anchor and the rest to go aloft and unfurl the sails. At the same time he warned the natives to withdraw, as the ship was going to sea. A fresh breeze was then springing up and in a few moments more their prey would have escaped them; but immediately on receiving this notice, by a preconcerted signal the Indians, with a terrific yell, drew forth the knives and war bludgeons they had concealed in their bundles of furs and rushed upon the crew of the ship.

Mr. Lewis was struck, and fell over a bale of blankets. Mr. McKay, however, was the first victim whom they sacrificed to their fury. Two savages, whom, from the crown of the poop where I was seated, I had seen follow this gentleman step by step, now cast themselves upon him, and having given him a blow on the head with a potumagan felled him to the deck, then took him up and flung him into the sea, where the women left in charge of the canoes quickly finished him with their paddles. Another set flung themselves upon the Captain, who defended himself for a long time with his pocket-knife, but, overpowered by numbers, perished also under the blows of these murderers. I next saw (and that was the last occurrence of which I was witness before quitting the ship) the sailors who were aloft slip down by the rigging and get below through the steerage hatchway. They were five, I think, in number, and one of them in descending received a knife-stab in the back. I then jumped overboard to escape a similar fate to that of the Captain and Mr. McKay. The women in the canoes, to whom I surrendered myself as a slave, took me in and bade me hide myself under some mats which were in the pirogues, which I did.

Soon after, I heard the discharge of firearms, immediately upon which the Indians fled from the vessel and pulled for the shore as fast as possible, nor did they venture to go alongside the ship again the whole of that day. The next day, having seen four men lower a boat and pull away from the ship, they sent some pirogues in chase: but whether those men were overtaken and murdered, or gained the open sea and perished there, I never could learn.

Nothing more was seen stirring on board the *Tonquin*; the natives pulled cautiously around her and some of the more daring went on board; at last, the savages, finding themselves absolute masters of the ship, rushed on board in a crowd to pillage her. But very soon, when there were about four or five hundred either huddled together on deck or clinging to the sides, all eager for plunder, the ship blew up with a horrible noise. "I was on the shore," said the Indian, "when the explosion took place, saw the great volume of smoke burst forth in the spot where the ship had been, and high in the air above, arms, legs, heads, and bodies flying in every direction. The tribe acknowledged a loss of over two hundred of their people on that occasion. As for me, I remained their prisoner, and have been their slave for two years. It is but now that I have been ransomed by my friends. I have told you the truth, and hope you will acquit me of having in any way participated in that bloody affair." [127]

Our Indian having finished his discourse, we made him presents proportioned to the melancholy satisfaction he had given us in communicating the true history of the sad fate of our former companions and to the trouble he had taken in coming to us; so that he returned apparently well satisfied with our liberality.

---

[127] This event was described in the Journal of Robert Stuart as follows: On the afternoon of August 11, a Tchinouk came to the American trading post and gave further details which left no more doubt. He heard them from other Indians recently from the country of the Niouetians. According to their account, the cause of the catastrophe should be blamed on Captain Thorn. He offered to give the Niouetians, having come on board to bargain, only two wool blankets for a marine otter pelt. The Indians were very displeased with the offer, and a chief spoke insolently to the captain, who hit him in the face with an otter pelt. The chief, enraged, returned all his people to shore. The following day, the *Tonquin* made sail for Noutka, behind about sixty boats of Niouetians. These boats had gone immediately after the incident to find the chief of Noutka, to request he join them. He agreed, and, the following day, they accosted the ship with furs. They traded two blankets and two knives per otter pelt, and everyone seemed satisfied. The trade with the Indians went briskly, and their number increased at every moment. At a given signal, four of them fell on Captain Thorn, and a fifth cut his throat. Others attacked Mr. Mackay, but he withdrew to the forecastle where, with his dagger, he furiously killed three of them. They nevertheless overcame him, and he received a blow in the face with a club, cutting him down. While this was going on, each man of the crew was attacked by two Indians and massacred, except for four sailors who went down into the powder stores and ignited them, heroically sacrificing their lives by blowing the ship up with a hundred savages still on board.

Captain Smith of the *Albatross*, who had seen the wreck of the *Tonquin*, in mentioning to us it's sad fate attributed the cause of the disaster to the rash conduct of a Captain Ayres of Boston. That navigator had taken off, as I have mentioned already, ten or a dozen natives of Newitte as hunters, with a promise of bringing them back to their country, which promise he inhumanly broke by leaving them on some desert islands in Sir Francis Drake's Bay. The countrymen of these unfortunates, indignant at the conduct of the American captain, had sworn to avenge themselves on the first white men who appeared among them. Chance willed it that our vessel was the first to enter that bay, and the natives but too well executed on our people their project of vengeance.

Whatever may have been the first and principal cause of this misfortune (for doubtless it is necessary to suppose more than one), seventeen white men and twelve Sandwich Islanders were massacred: not one escaped from the butchery to bring us the news of it, but the Indian of Gray's Harbor. The massacre of our people was avenged, it is true, by the destruction often times the number of their murderers; but this circumstance, which could perhaps gladden the heart of a savage, was a feeble consolation (if it was any) for civilized men. The death of Mr. Alexander Mc-Kay was an irreparable loss to the Company, which would probably have been dissolved by the remaining partners but for the arrival of the energetic Mr. Hunt. Interesting as was the recital of the Indian of Gray's Harbor throughout, when he came to the unhappy end of that estimable man marks of regret were visibly painted on the countenances of all who listened.

At the beginning of September, Mr. McKenzie set off with Messrs. Wallace and Seton to carry a supply of goods to the gentlemen wintering in the interior, as well as to inform them of the arrangements concluded with Mr. Hunt and to enjoin them to send down all their furs and all the Sandwich Islanders, that the former might be shipped for America and the latter sent back to their country.

Franchere's Journal

A Voyage to the Northwest Coast of America

Chapter Ten

The Surrender of Astoria

A few days after Mr. McKenzie left us we were greatly surprised by the appearance of two canoes bearing the British flag, with a third between them carrying the flag of the United States, all rounding Tongue Point. It was no other than Mr. McKenzie himself, returning with Messrs. J. G. McTavish and Angus Bethune[128] of the North West Company. He had met these gentlemen near the first rapids, and had determined to return with them to the establishment in con-

---

[128] Angus Bethume appears as one of the chief members of Alexander Henry's party in Saskatchewan country. After reaching Astoria with McTavish in 1813, he remained in the Columbia country until April, 1817, when he left Fort George with a brigade which set out for Fort Williams. He later was supercargo on North West Company's vessel *Columbia,* sailing from the Columbia River to China. (*Franchere's Narrative*)

sequence of information which they gave him. Those gentlemen were in light canoes (i. e., without any lading) and formed the vanguard to a flotilla of eight, loaded with furs, under the conduct of Messrs. John Stuart and McMillan[129].

Mr. McTavish[130] came to our quarters at the factory and showed Mr. McDougall a letter which had been addressed to the latter by Mr. Angus Shaw, his uncle, and one of the partners of the North West Company. Mr. Shaw informed his nephew that the ship *Isaac Todd* had sailed from London with letters of marque in the month of March, in company with the frigate *Phoebe*, having orders from the government to seize our establishment, which had been represented to the Lords of the Admiralty as an important colony

---

[129] A. McMillan was a member of a party organized at Fort Williams by John McDonald in 1808 or 1809 for relief of David Thompson, the scientist of the North West Company, then in the Rocky Mountains. McMillan was with Thompson until the spring of 1810 when he joined Alexander Henry. July 9 of the same year, McMillan set out for the Columbia to watch the operations there of Hudson's Bay Company, but was prevented by the Indians from establishing a post, and rejoined Henry the following January. In 1812 he was in charge of North West Company's house near Spokane Falls. (*Franchere's Narrative*)

[130] McTavish had previously been to Fort Astoria under false pretences and had be treated very cordially, feed and supplied. This time he revealed the true purpose of his visits.

founded by the American government. The eight canoes left behind came up, meanwhile, and uniting themselves to the others they formed a camp of about seventy-five men at the bottom of a little bay or cove near our factory. As they were destitute of provisions we supplied them; but Messrs. McDougall and McKenzie affecting to dread a surprise from this British force under our guns, we kept strictly on our guard; for we were inferior in point of numbers, although our position was exceedingly advantageous.

As the season advanced and their ship did not arrive our new neighbors found themselves in a very disagreeable situation, without food, or merchandise wherewith to procure it from the natives; viewed by the latter with a distrustful and hostile eye, as being our enemies and therefore exposed to attack and plunder on their part with impunity; supplied with good hunters, indeed, but wanting ammunition to render their skill available. Weary, at length, of applying to us incessantly for food (which we furnished them with a sparing hand) unable either to retrace their steps through the wilderness or to remain in their present position, they came to the conclusion of proposing to buy of us the whole establishment.

Placed as we were in the situation of expecting, day by day, the arrival of an English ship-of-war to seize upon all we possessed, we listened to their propositions. Several meetings and discussions took place; the negotiations were protracted by the hope of one party that the long-expected armed force would arrive, to render the purchase unnecessary, and were urged forward by the other in order to conclude the affair before that occurrence should intervene; at length the price of the goods and furs in the factory was agreed upon, and the bargain was signed by both parties on the 23d of October. The gentlemen of the North West Company took possession of Astoria, agreeing to pay the servants of the Pacific Fur Company (the name which had been chosen by Mr. Astor) the arrears of their wages, to be deducted from the price of the goods which we delivered, to supply them with provisions, and give a free passage to those who wished to return to Canada overland. The American colors were hauled down from the factory and the British up, to the no small chagrin and mortification of those who were American citizens.[131]

It was thus that after having passed the seas and suffered all sorts of fatigues and privations I lost in a moment all my hopes of fortune. I could not help remarking that we had no right to expect such treatment on the part of the British government, after the assurances we had received from Mr. Jackson, His Majesty's charge d'affaires previous to our departure from New York[132]. But as I have just intimated, the agents

---

[131] When the War of 1812 broke out, the North West Company took advantage of the situation to persuade the American F Company to sell out its interest in Columbia region. F.M. Buckland tells us that Duncan MacDougall, the Factor in charge, agreed to the price of $80,500 (O.H.S. Report No. 17, page 74). Both Fort Astoria, renamed Fort George, and Fort Okanogan be-came North West posts until 1821 when they became Hudson's Bay Company post upon the amalgamation of the two great fur trading companies. The expense of building Mr. Astor's esta-blishment at Astoria, including those at Okanagon and Spokan, with boats, *bateaux*, tools, cannon, munitions, goods, transpor-tation and salaries of clerks and men, etc., etc., was near two hundred thousand dollars, for which he received in bills on Mon-treal about forty thousand, including the appraised value of the furs at the fort, which was thirty-six thousand eight hundred and thirty-five dollars and fifty cents.

[132] Before leaving New York, it is well to observe that during our stay in that city, Mr. McKay thought it the part of prudence to have an inter-view with the minister plenipotentiary of his Britannic majesty, Mr. Jackson, to inform him of the object of our voyage, and get his views in regard to the line of conduct we ought to follow in case of war breaking out between the two powers; intimating to him that we were all British subjects, and were about to trade under the American flag. After some

of the North West Company had exaggerated the importance of the factory in the eyes of the British Ministry; for if the latter had known what it really was a mere trading-post and that nothing but the rivalry of the fur-traders of the North West Company was interested in its destruction, they would never have taken umbrage at it, or at least would never have sent a maritime expedition to destroy it. The sequel will show that I was not mistaken in this opinion.

The greater part of the servants of the Pacific Fur Company entered the sendee of the Company of the North West: the rest preferred to return to their country, and I was of the number of these last.

Nevertheless, Mr. McTavish, after many ineffectual attempts to persuade me to remain with them, having intimated that the establishment could not dispense with my services as I was the only person who could assist them in their trade,

---

moments of reflection Mr. Jackson told him, "that we were going on a very hazardous enterprise; that he saw our object was purely commercial, and that all he could promise us, was, that in case of a war we should be respected as British subjects and traders."This reply appeared satisfactory, and Mr. McKay thought we had nothing to apprehend on that side.

127

especially for provisions, of which they would soon be in the greatest need, I agreed with them (without however relinquishing my previous engagement with Mr. Astor's agents) for five months, that is to say, till the departure of the expedition which was to ascend the Columbia in the spring, and reach Canada by way of the Rocky Mountains and the rivers of the interior.

Messrs. John Stuart and McKenzie set off about the end of this month for the interior in order that the latter might make over to the former the posts established on the *Spokan* and *Okenakan* rivers.

On the 15th of November Messrs. Alexander Stuart and Alexander Henry, both partners of the N. W. Company, arrived at the factory in a couple of bark canoes manned by sixteen voyagers. They had set out from Fort William on Lake Superior in the month of July. They brought us Canadian papers, by which we learned that Alexander Ross states that Franchere was the only clerk who disclosed a willingness to join the North West Company. He was a Canadian from Montreal, and in those days the North West stood high in Canada, and particularly in Montreal.

On the morning of the 30th we saw a large vessel standing in under Cape Disappointment (which proved in this instance to deserve its name); and soon after that vessel came to anchor in Baker Bay. Not knowing whether it was a friendly or a hostile sail, we thought it prudent to send on board Mr. McDougall in a canoe manned by such of the men as had been previously in the service of the Pacific Fur Company, with injunctions to declare themselves Americans if the vessel was American, and Englishmen in the contrary case. While this party was on its way, Mr. McTavish caused all the furs which were marked with the initials of the N. W. Company to be placed on board the two barges at the Fort and sent them up the river above Tongue Point, where they were to wait for a concerted signal that was to inform them whether the new comers were friends or foes. Toward midnight Mr. Halsey who had accompanied Mr. McDougall to the vessel, returned to the Fort and announced to us that she was the British sloop-of-war *Raccoon* of

26 guns, commanded by Captain Black, with a complement of 120 men, fore and aft. Mr. John McDonald, a partner of the N. W. Company, was a passenger on the *Raccoon*, with five voyagers, destined for the Company's service. He had left England in the frigate *Phoebe*[133], which had sailed in company with the *Isaac Todd* as far as Rio Ja-neiro; but there falling in with the British squadron, the admiral changed the destination of the frigate dispatching the sloops-of-war *Raccoon* and *Cherub* to convoy the *Isaac Todd* and sent the *Phoebe* to search for the American Commodore Porter, who was then on the Pacific capturing all the British whalers and other trading vessels he met with. These four vessels then sailed in company as far as Cape Horn, where they parted, after agreeing on the island of Juan Fernandez as a rendezvous. The three ships-of-war met, in fact, at that island; but after having a long time waited in vain for the *Isaac Todd*, Commodore Hillyar who commanded this little squadron, hearing of the injury inflicted by

---

[133] HMS *Phoebe* was a 36-gun the British Royal Navy. She had a career of almost twenty years and fought in the French Revolutionary Wars, the Napoleonic Wars and the War of 1812.

Commodore Porter on the British commerce, and especially on the whalers who frequent these seas, resolved to go in quest of him in order to give him combat;[134] and retaining the *Cherub* to assist him, detailed the *Raccoon* to go and destroy the American establishment on the river Co-

---

[134] Commodore James Hillyar got his opportunity to give Commodore Porter and the *Essex* "combat." Hillyar with the *Phoebe* and *Cherub* found David Porter with the *Essex* and *Essex Jr.* in the neutral port of Valparaiso, Chile. In the *Memoir of Commodore David Porter*; "in their next meeting he and Capt. Porter talked over amicably the object of the former in coming to the Pacific, his long hunt after the *Essex* and his desire to know what Porter intended to do with his prizes, &c. Capt. Porter informed Hillyar, that he intended to burn them and that whenever he sent away the *Cherub*, he intended to go to sea, and would take the first opportunity, when the *Essex* could meet the *Phoebe* alone, of testing the force of the two ships; that as the *Essex* was much the smaller vessel of the two, he did not feel justified in challenging the *Phoebe* to fight, but that if Capt. Hillyar would send away the *Cherub*, he would have no hesitation in engaging him." Intercourse between the two commanders continued. An agreement was reached to release the prisoners on the British whalers captured by Porter for the release of an equal number of American prisoners in England. James Hillyar was given several opportunities to combat the *Essex* but would not do so without the British *Cherub* joining the battle as well. After much maneuvering the two British ship were able to join the *Essex* in battle and defeated her. The *Essex* tried to escape on March 28, and when extremely close to success, she lost a topmast, impairing maneuverability. A few hours later, Hillyar with the *Phoebe* and *Cherub* brought *Essex* and the *Essex Junior* to battle. For hours, the *Essex*, armed with carronades, cannons with short range, was pounded by the long cannons of *Phoebe* and *Cherub*, until the ship was an unmanageable wreck and surrendered. Out of a crew of 154 the *Essex* suffered 58 dead, 45 wounded and 31 missing. The *Phoebe* had 4 killed and 7 wounded. The *Cherub* had 1 killed and 3 wounded. David Glasgow Farragut, a future United States Admiral, was on board the *Essex* as a midshipman during this battle. There is a memorial for the American dead in the Dissidents Cemetery in Valparaiso.

lumbia, being assured by Mr. McDonald that a single sloop-of-war would be sufficient for that service.

Mr. McDonald had consequently embarked with his people on board the *Raccoon*. This gentleman informed us that they had experienced frightful weather in doubling the Cape, and that he entertained serious apprehensions for the safety of the *Isaac Todd*, but that if she was safe we might expect her to arrive in the river in two or three weeks. The signal gun agreed upon having been fired, for the return of the barges, Mr. McTavish came back to the Fort with the furs and was overjoyed to learn of the arrival of Mr. McDonald.

On the 1st of December the *Raccoon*'s brig came up to the fort[135], bringing Mr. McDonald[136]

---

[135] Chief Comcomly also arrived with some excellent salmon and the meat of a large biche. There came with him a half-breed "off-spring of a ship, immortalized as a mirror of ugliness. He was a perfected *lusus naturaes*, and his history was rather curious. His skin was fair, his face partially freckled and his hair was quite red. He was about five feet ten inches tall, was slender, but remarkably well made: his head had not undergone the flattening process, and he was called Jack Ramsey in consequence of that name being punctured on his left arm. The Indians allege that his father was an English Sailor who deserted from a trading vessel, and had lived for many years among their tribe, one of whom he married; when Jack was born he insisted on preserving the child's head in its natural state, and while young punctured the arm in the above

surnamed *Bras Creche*, (or crooked arm) and the first lieutenant, Mr. Sheriff. Both these gentlemen were convalescent from the effects of an accident which had happened to them in the passage between Juan Fernandez and the mouth of the Columbia. The Captain, wishing to clean the guns, ordered them to be scaled, that is, fired off: during this exercise one of the guns hung fire; the sparks fell into a cartridge tub and setting fire to the combustibles, communicated also to some priming horns suspended above; an ex-

---

manner. Old Ramsey died about twenty years before this period; he had several children but Jack was the only red-headed one among them. (Alexander Henry and David Thompson, *The Saskatchewan and Columbia Rivers*). A December 31, 1805 entry in the Journal of Lewis and Clark also refer to Jack Ramsey: With the party of Clatsop who visited us last was a man of much lighter colored than the natives are generally. He was freckled with long dusky red hair about 25 years of age and most certainly be half white at least. He appeared to understand more of the English language than the others of his party but did not speak a word of English. He possessed all the habits of the Indians. As we could not obtain an ac-count of his origin, we concluded that one of his parents, at least, must have been white. He was probably the man to have later been known as Jack Ramsay, as was tattooed on his left arm.

[136] John McDonald of Garth had a crocked arm caused by an accident. He was a Scotch Highlander who came to Canada in 1791 at the age of 17. He was in the western county, chiefly Saskatchewan from 1791 until 1812. In the latter year he returned to England but left in February, 1813, for the Columbia River. He was in a party with Franchere which left Fort George April 4, 1814. In 1816 McDonald retired from the company and settled in Northern Canada where he lived until 1860. In 1859 he wrote a brief sketch of his life; *Les Bourgeois de la Champagnie du Nord-Ouest*. Quebec, 1890. (*Franchere's Narrative*)

plosion followed, which reached some twenty persons; eight were killed on the spot, the rest were severely burned; Messrs. McDonald and Sheriff had suffered a great deal; it was with difficulty that their clothes had been removed; and when the Lieutenant came ashore, he had not recovered the use of his hands. Among the killed was an American named Flatt, who was in the service of the North West Company and whose loss these gentlemen appeared exceedingly to regret[137].

As there were goods[138] destined for the Company on board the HMS *Raccoon*[139], the schooner *Dolly* was sent to Baker Bay to bring them up: but the weather was so bad and the wind so violent that she did not return till the 12th, bringing up, together with the goods, Captain Black, a lieutenant of marines, four soldiers, and as many

---

[137] This gunnery exercise, no doubt put on for the benefit of the residents of Fort Astoria, killed eight people on board the HMS *Raccoon* and wounded 20 others.

[138] Pieces of goods landed at Astoria from the HMS *Raccoon*: 7 bales of blankets, 11 shrouds, 2 sundries, 8 guns, 14 power, 17 ball and shot, tobacco 11, Brazil tobacco 1, kettles 10, shirts, etc. 2, flints etc. 2, beads etc. 2. 87 pieces in all plus 3 kegs of beef belonging to the *Isaac Todd*.

[139] The HMS *Raccoon* was an 18-gun sloop launched in 1808.

sailors. We entertained our guests as splendidly as it lay in our power to do. After dinner the Captain caused firearms to be given to the servants of the Company and we all marched under arms to the square or platform, where a flagstaff had been erected. There the Captain took a British Union Jack, which he had brought on shore for the occasion, and caused it to be run up to the top of the staff; then, taking a bottle of Madeira wine, he broke it on the flag-staff, declaring in a loud voice that he took possession of the establishment and of the country in the name of His Britannic Majesty; and changed the name of Astoria to Fort George. Some few Indian chiefs had been got together to witness this ceremony and I explained to them in their own language what it signified. Three rounds of artillery and musketry were fired and the health of the king was drunk by the parties interested, according to the usage on like occasions.[140]

---

[140] In Henry and Thompson's journal we find that the Captain did not arrive until 11 p.m. on the 12th after groping his way along the beach afoot in palpable darkness no doubt swearing like a private every time he slipped on a stone, stepped in a puddle or stumbled over a stump; that they got supper for him and made a wet night of it until 2 a.m. before they went to bed. So it was not

The sloop being detained by contrary winds, the Captain caused an exact survey to be made of the entrance of the river, as well as of the navigable channel between Baker Bay and Fort George.

The officers visited the fort, turn about, and seemed to me in general very much dissatisfied with their fool's errand, as they called it: they had expected to find a number of American vessels loaded with rich furs, and had calculated in advance their share in the booty of Astoria. They had not met a vessel, and their astonishment was at its height when they saw that our establishment had been transferred to the North West Company and was under the British flag. It will suffice to quote a single expression of Captain Black's in order to show how much they were deceived in their expectations. The Captain landed after dark ; when we showed him the next morning the palisades and log bastions of the factory, he inquired if there was not another fort; on being assured that there was no other he

---

until the 13th that they "spliced the main brace" for the performance.

cried out, with an air of the greatest astonishment: "What! is this the fort which was represented to me as so formidable! Good God! I could batter it down in two hours with a four-pounder!"

There were on board the *Raccoon* two young men from Canada who had been impressed at Quebec when that vessel was there some years before her voyage to the Columbia: one of them was named Parent, a blacksmith, and was of Quebec: the other was from Upper Canada, and was named McDonald. These young persons signified to us that they would be glad to remain at Fort George: and as there was among our men some who would gladly have shipped, we proposed to the Captain an exchange, but he would not consent to it. John Little, a boat builder from New York, who had been on the sick list a long time, was sent on board and placed under the care of the sloop's surgeon, Mr. O'Brien, the Captain engaging to land him at the Sandwich Islands. P. D. Jeremie also shipped himself as under clerk. The vessel hoisted sail and got out under clerk. The vessel hoisted sail of the river on the 31st of December.[141]

From the account given in this chapter the reader will see with what facility the establishment of the Pacific Fur Company could have escaped capture by the British force. It was only necessary to get rid of the land party of the North West Company who were completely in our power then remove our effects up the river upon some small stream, and await the result.

The sloop-of-war arrived, it is true; but as, in the case I suppose, she would have found nothing, she would have left, after setting fire to our deserted houses. None of their boats would have dared follow us.

---

[141] **The Oregon Encyclopedia notes:** Captain Black soon made preparations to sail for Hawaii to hunt for American ships. On December 31, when the *Raccoon* crossed the Columbia's treacherous bar, the ship struck its bottom twice and lost a portion of the keel. With water pouring in and men frantically working the pumps night and day, the *Raccoon* made instead for the coast of California, arriving at the Spanish colony of San Francisco on January 14. There, with the help of the *Isaac Todd*, which had fortuitously appeared in the area, the *Raccoon* was repaired and continued its activities in the Pacific. The HMS *Raccoon* was decommissioned and sold in 1838. In 1973, the twelve-foot section of the sloop's keel that had been lost on the Columbia in 1813 washed ashore. It is currently on display at the Columbia River Maritime Museum in Astoria.

Franchere's Journal

A Voyage to the Northwest Coast of America

Chapter Eleven
Indian Treachery and Warfare

ON the 3d of January, 1814 two canoes laden with merchandise for the interior were dispatched under the command of Mr. Alexander and Mr. James Keith,[142] with fifteen men under them. Two of the latter were charged with letters for the posts (of the North West Company) east of the mountains, containing instructions to the persons in superintendence there to have in readiness canoes and the requisite provisions for a large party intending to go east the ensuing

---

[142] James Keith winters on the Columbia in 1813-1814. In the middle of March 1814 he leaves Fort George and goes on an overland tour. Returning, he left Fort George again Aug. 5 and was at Fort Okanagan Aug. 23-27, and went over the Rocky Mountains with dispatches. Returning to Fort George Nov. 8. (Henry and Thompson Journals)

spring. I took this opportunity of advising my friends in Canada of my intention to return home that season. It was the third attempt I had made to send news of my existence to my relatives and friends: the first two had miscarried and this was doomed to meet the same fate.

Messrs. J. Stuart and McKenzie, who (as was seen in a previous chapter) had been sent to notify the gentlemen in the interior of what had taken place at Astoria, and to transfer the wintering posts to the North West Company, returned to Fort George on the morning of the 6th. They stated that they had left Messrs. Clarke and D. Stuart behind with the loaded canoes, and also that the party had been attacked by the natives above the Falls.

As they were descending the river toward evening, between the first and second portages, they had espied a large number of Indians congregated at no great distance in the prairie, which gave them some uneasiness. In fact, sometime after they had encamped, and when all the people were asleep, except Mr. Stuart who was on guard, these savages had stealthily approached

the camp and discharged some arrows, one of which had penetrated the coverlet of one of the men who was lying near the baggage and had pierced the cartilage of his ear; the pain made him utter a sharp cry, which alarmed the whole camp and threw it into an uproar. The natives, perceiving it, fled to the woods, howling and yelling like so many demons. In the morning our people picked up eight arrows round the camp:[143] they could yet hear the savages yell and whoop in the woods: but notwithstanding, the party reached the lower end of the portage unmolested.

The audacity which these barbarians had displayed in attacking a party of from forty to forty-five persons made us suppose that they would much more probably attack the party of Mr. Stuart, which was composed of but seventeen men. Consequently I received orders to get ready

---

[143] The arrows found in camp were recognized as those used by Fall Indian (of the Columbia), three of them being of reeds with wood points; the others being of plain wood; none were shod with iron or bone; they appeared to be boy's arrows. About two hours before daylight two men were seen skulking near the camp, our people fired at them but to no effect. Sometime before day light there was a great whooping and hallooing above and below us. (Henry and Thompson Journals)

forthwith a canoe and firearms in order to proceed to their relief. The whole was ready in the short space of two hours, and I embarked immediately with a guide and eight men. Our instructions were to use all possible diligence to overtake Messrs. Stewart and Keith, and to convey them to the upper end of the last portage; or to return with the goods, if we met too much resistance on the part of the natives. We travelled, then, all that day and all the night of the 6th, and on the 7th till evening. Finding ourselves then at a little distance from the Rapids, I came to a halt to put the firearms in order and let the men take some repose. About midnight I caused them to re-embark, and ordered the men to sing as they rowed, that the party whom we wished to overtake might hear us as we passed, if perchance they were encamped on some one of the islands of which the river is full in this part. In fact, we had hardly proceeded five or six miles when we were hailed by someone, apparently in the middle of the stream. We stopped rowing and answered, and were soon joined by our people of the expedition, who were all descending the river

in a canoe. They informed us that they had been attacked the evening before and that Mr. Stuart had been wounded. We turned about and all proceeded in company toward the fort. In the morning, when we stopped to breakfast, Mr. Keith[144] gave me the particulars of the affair of the day preceding.

Having arrived at the foot of the Rapids, they commenced the portage on the south bank of the river, which is obstructed with boulders over which it was necessary to pass the effects. After they had hauled over the two canoes and a part of the goods the natives approached in great numbers, trying to carry off something unobserved. Mr. Stuart was at the upper end of the portage (the portage being about six hundred yards in length) and Mr. Keith accompanied the loaded men. An Indian seized a bag containing articles of little value and fled: Mr. Stuart, who saw the act, pursued the thief and after some resistance on the latter's part succeeded in making him relinquish his booty. Immediately he saw a number of Indians armed with bows and ar-

---

[144] James Keith was a clerk who had arrived in Astoria November 15, 1813 with Alexander Henry and Alexander Stewart.

rows approaching him: one of them bent his bow and took aim; Mr. Stuart, on his part, leveled his gun at the Indian, warning the latter not to shoot, and at the same instant received an arrow which pierced his left shoulder. He then drew the trigger; but as it had rained all day the gun missed fire and before he could re-prime another arrow, better aimed than the first, struck him in the left side and penetrated between two of his ribs in the region of the heart, and would have proved fatal, no doubt, but for a stone-pipe he had fortunately in his side-pocket, and which was broken by the arrow; at the same moment his gun was discharged and the Indian fell dead. Several others then rushed forward to avenge the death of their compatriot; but two of the men came up with their loads and their gun (for these portages were made arms in hand) and seeing what was going forward one of them threw his pack on the ground, fired on one of the Indians, and brought him down. He got up again, however, and picked up his weapons, but the other man ran upon him, wrested from him his war-club, and dispatched him by repeated blows on the head with it. The other savages, seeing the bulk of our people approaching the scene of combat, retired and crossed the river. In the mean time, Mr. Stuart extracted the arrows from his body by the aid of one of the men : the blood flowed in abundance from the wounds and he saw that it would be impossible for him to pursue his journey; he therefore gave orders for the canoes and goods to be carried back to the lower end of the portage. Presently they saw a great number of pirogues full of warriors coming from the opposite side of the river. Our people then considered that they could do nothing better than to get away as fast as possible; they contrived to transport over one canoe in which they all embarked, abandoning the other and the goods to the natives. While the barbarians were plundering these effects, more precious in their estimation than the apples of gold in the garden of the Hesperides, our party retired and got out of sight.

The retreat was, notwithstanding, so precipitate, that they left behind an Indian from the Lake of the Two Mountains who was in the service of the Company as a hunter. This Indian had persisted in concealing himself behind the rocks, meaning, he said, to kill some of those thieves, and did not return in time for the embarkation. Mr. Keith regretted this brave man's obstinacy, fearing, with good reason, that he would be discovered and murdered by the natives. We rowed all that day and night and reached the factory on the 9th at sunrise. Our first care, after having announced the misfortune of our people, was to dress the wounds of Mr. Stuart, which had been merely bound with a wretched piece of cotton cloth.

The goods which had been abandoned were of consequence to the Company, inasmuch as they could not be replaced. It was dangerous, besides, to leave the natives in possession of some fifty guns and a considerable quantity of ammunition, which they might use against us. The partners, therefore, decided to fit out an expedition immediately to chastise the robbers, or at least to endeavor to recover the goods. I went, by their order, to find the principal chiefs of the neighboring tribes, to explain to them what had taken place and invite them to join us, to which they willingly consented. Then, having got ready six canoes, we re-embarked on the 10th to the number of sixty-two men, all armed from head to foot, and provided with a small brass field-piece.[145]

We soon reached the lower end of the first rapid: but the essential thing was wanting to our little force; it was without provisions; our first care then was to try to procure these. Having arrived opposite a village, we perceived on the bank about thirty armed savages who seemed to await us firmly. As it was not our policy to seem bent on hostilities, we landed on the opposite bank and I crossed the river with five or six men to enter into parley with them and try to obtain provisions. I immediately became aware that the village was abandoned, the women and children having fled to the woods, taking with them all the particles of food. The young men, however, offered us dogs, of which we purchased a score. Then we passed to a second village, where they were already informed of our coming. Here we bought forty-five dogs and a horse. With this

---

[145] Artillery

stock we formed an encampment on an island called Strawberry Island[146].

Seeing ourselves now provided with food for several days, we informed the natives touching the motives which had brought us, and announced to them that we were determined to put them all to death and burn their villages if they did not bring back in two days the effects stolen on the 7th. A party was detached to the Rapids, where the attack on Mr. Stuart had taken place. We found the villages all deserted. Crossing to the north bank we found a few natives, of whom we made inquiries respecting the Nipissing Indian who had been left behind, but they assured us that they had seen nothing of him.[147]

---

[146] When the Lewis and Clark expedition was traveling to the Pacific Ocean they reached the head of the Cascades on the Columbia River. Clark, accompanied by Joe Fields, walked ahead to view the rapids. They went as far as Beacon Rock, where the tide-water was noticed. On that day, October 31, 1805, they picked strawberries on what was later known as Hamilton, just below where Bonneville dam was constructed. They gave it the name of Strawberry Island. (J.Nelson Berry)

[147] This Indian returned some time after to the factory, but in a pitiable condition. After the departure of the canoe he had concealed himself behind a rock, and so passed the night. At day-break, fearing to be discovered, he gained the woods and directed his steps toward the fort, across a mountainous region. He arrived at length at the bank of a little stream, which he was at first unable to cross. Hunger, in the meantime, began to urge him; he might have appeased it with game, of which he saw plenty, but unfortunately he had lost the flint of his gun. At last, with a raft of sticks, he crossed the river and arrived at a village, the in-

Not having succeeded in recovering, above the Rapids, any part of the lost goods, the inhabitants all protesting that it was not they, but the villages below, which had perpetrated the robbery, we descended the river again and re-encamped on Strawberry Island. As the intention of the partners was to intimidate the natives, without (if possible) shedding blood, we made a display of our numbers and from time to time fired off our little field-piece to let them see that we could reach them from one side of the river to the other. The Indian Coalpo and his wife, who had accompanied us, advised us to make prisoner one of the chiefs. We succeeded in this design, without incurring any danger. Having invited one of the natives to come and smoke with us, he came accordingly: a little after, came another; at last, one of the chiefs, and he one of the most considered among them, also came.

Being notified secretly of his character by Coalpo, who was concealed in the tent, we seized him forthwith, tied him to a stake, and placed a

habitants of which disarmed him and made him prisoner. Our people hearing where he was, sent to seek him, and gave some blankets for his ransom. Bibaud.

149

guard over him with a naked sword, as if ready to cut his head off on the least attempt being made by his people for his liberation. The other Indians were then suffered to depart with the news for his tribe that unless the goods were brought to us in twenty-four hours their chief would be put to death. Our stratagem succeeded: soon after we heard wailing and lamentation in the village and they presently brought us part of the guns, some brass kettles, and a variety of smaller articles, protesting that this was all their share of the plunder. Keeping our chief as a hostage, we passed to the other village and succeeded in recovering the rest of the guns and about a third of the other goods.

Although they had been the aggressors, yet as they had had two men killed and we had not lost any on our side we thought it our duty to conform to the usage of the country and abandon to them the remainder of the stolen effects, to cover, according to their expression, the bodies of their two slain compatriots. Besides, we began to find ourselves short of provisions, and it would not have been easy to get at our enemies to punish them if they had taken refuge in the woods, according to their custom when they feel themselves the weaker party. So we released our prisoner and gave him a flag, telling him that when he presented it unfurled we should regard it as a sign of peace and friendship: but if, when we were passing the portage, any one of the natives should have the misfortune to come near the baggage we would kill him on the spot. We reembarked on the 19th and on the 22d reached the fort, where we made a report of our martial expedition. We found Mr. Stuart very ill of his wounds, especially of the one in the side, which was so much swelled that we had every reason to think the arrow had been poisoned.[148]

If we did not do the savages as much harm as we might have done, it was not from timidity but from humanity, and in order not to shed human blood uselessly. For after all, what good would it have done us to have slaughtered some of these barbarians, whose crime was not the effect of de-

---

[148] The Nez Perce sometimes used dried rattlesnake venom on their arrow heads, the poultices may have been as effective as Seton believed them to have been, but the drying of venom also weakens its potency considerably. (Seton)

pravity and wickedness, but of an ardent and irresistible desire to ameliorate their condition?

It must be allowed also that the interest, well understood, of the partners of the North West Company was opposed to too strongly marked acts of hostility on their part: it behooved them exceedingly not to make irreconcilable enemies of the populations neighboring on the portages of the Columbia, which they would so often be obliged to pass and repass in the future. It is also probable that the other natives on the banks, as well as of the river as of the sea, would not have seen with indifference their countrymen too signally or too rigorously punished by strangers; and that they would have made common cause with the former to resist the latter, and perhaps even to drive them from the country.

I must not omit to state that all the firearms surrendered by the Indians on this occasion were found loaded with ball and primed, with a little piece of cotton laid over the priming to keep the powder dry. This shows how soon they would acquire the use of guns, and how careful traders should be in intercourse with strange Indians not to teach them their use.

Franchere's Journal

A Voyage to the Northwest Coast of America

Chapter Twelve
Preparations for Crossing the Continent

The new proprietors of our establishment, being dissatisfied with the site we had chosen,
came to the determination to change it; after sur-
veying both sides of the river, they found no better place than the headland which we had
named Tongue point. This point, or to speak
more accurately, perhaps, this cape, extends
about a quarter of a mile into the river, being
connected with the mainland by a low, narrow
neck, over which the Indians, in stormy weather,
haul their canoes in passing up and down the
river; and terminating in an almost perpendi-
cular rock, of about 250 or 300 feet elevation.

This bold summit was covered with a dense

forest of pine trees; the ascent from the lower neck was gradual and easy; it abounded in springs of the finest water; on either side it had a cove to shelter the boats necessary for a trading establishment. This peninsula had truly the appearance of a huge tongue. Astoria had been built nearer the ocean, but the advantages offered by Tongue point more than compensated for its greater distance. Its soil, in the rainy season, could be drained with little or no trouble; it was a better position to guard against attacks on the part of the natives, and less exposed to that of civilized enemies by sea or land in time of war.

All the hands who had returned from the interior, added to those who were already at the Fort, consumed, in an incredibly short space of time the small stock of provisions which had been conveyed by the Pacific Fur Company to the Company of the Northwest. It became a matter of necessity, therefore, to seek some spot where a part, at least, could be sent to subsist. With these views I left the fort on the 7th February with a number of men, belonging to the old concern, and who had refused to enter the service of the new one, to proceed to the establishment on the *Willamette* River,[149] under the charge of Mr. Alexander Henry, who had with him a number of first rate hunters. Leaving the Columbia to ascend the *Willamette*, I found the banks on either side of that stream well wooded, but low and swampy, until I reached the first falls; having passed which, by making a portage, I commenced ascending a clear but moderately deep channel, against a swift current. The banks on either side were bordered with forest trees, but behind that narrow belt, diversified with prairie, the landscape was magnificent; the hills were of moderate elevation, and rising in an amphitheatre. Deer and elk are found here in great abundance; and the post in charge of Mr. Henry had

---

[149] The Willamette Trading Post or Willamette Fur Post was a fur trade facility owned by the North West Company established near the Willamette River in what would become the French Prairie in. Established around 1813, the post was a small fur station where trappers working in the Willamette Valley could exchange their pelts and hides for other trade goods. It was built southeast of the current city of Newberg on the eastern shore of the river. The location was a few miles west of Champoeg. Built as a trade depot, the post was used by the North West Company for trading and as a game relay spot in support of their main outpost Fort George. The Willamette Trading Post remained in use until the mid-1830s. In later years, former North West Company employee Pierre Belleque settled a land claim and began farming at the site around 1833. He lived in the former building for a time, as his wife was related to an Hudson's Bay Company officer.

been established with a view of keeping constantly there a number of hunters to prepare dried venison for the use of the factory. On our arrival at the Columbia, considering the latitude, we had expected severe winter weather, such as is experienced in the same latitudes east; but we were soon undeceived; the mildness of the climate never permitted us to transport fresh provisions from the Willamette to Astoria. We had not a particle of salt; and the attempts we made to smoke or dry the venison proved abortive.

Having left the men under my charge with Mr. Henry, I took leave of that gentleman, and returned. At Oak Point I found Messrs. Keith and Pillet encamped, to pass there the season of sturgeon-fishing. They informed me that I was to stay with them.

Accordingly I remained at Oak Point the rest of the winter, occupied in trading with the Indians spread all along the river for some 30 or 40 miles above, in order to supply the factory with provisions. I used to take a boat with four or five men, visit every fishing station, trade for as much fish as would load the boat, and send her down to the fort. The surplus fish traded in the interval between the departure and return of the boat, was cut up, salted and barreled for future use. The salt had been recently obtained from a quarter to be presently mentioned.

About the middle of March Messrs. Keith and Pillet both left me and returned to the fort. Being now alone, I began seriously to reflect on my position, and it was in this interval that I positively decided to return to Canada. I made inquiries of the men sent up with the boats for fish, concerning the preparations for departure, but whether they had been enjoined secrecy, or were unwilling to communicate, I could learn nothing of what was doing below.

At last I heard that on the 28th February a sail had appeared at the mouth of the river. The gentlemen of the N.W. Company at first flattered themselves that it was the vessel they had so long expected. They were soon undeceived by a letter from Mr. Hunt, which was brought to the fort by the Indians of *Baker's bay*. That gentleman had purchased at the Marquesas islands a brig called The *Pedlar.*[150] it was on that vessel that he arrived, having for pilot Captain Northrop, formerly commander of the ship *Lark.*[151] The latter vessel had been outfitted by Mr. Astor, and dispatched from New York, in spite of the blockading squadron, with supplies for the *cidevant* Pacific Fur Company; but unhappily she had been assailed by a furious tempest and capsized in lat. 16° N., and three or four hundred miles from the Sandwich Islands. The mate who was sick, was drowned in the cabin, and four of the crew perished at the same time. The captain had

---

[150] An American Brig owned by Oliver Keating of Boston and commanded by George Clark. She was there in 1812 and in 1813 reached the Hawaiian Islands and there she was purchased on January 22nd, 1814 or February 8, 1814 by William Price Hunt for the Astoria venture. He placed Captain Northrup in command and the *Pedlar* sailed for the Columbia, when she arrived February 28 or March 5, 1814. On April 2, 1814 the *Pedlar* sailed from the Columbia River for Sitka, bearing some of the adventuers of Astoria.

[151] The *Lark*, of Astor's line, sailed from New York March 16, 1813. She encountered bad weather near the Island and after buffeting with storms for many days became "a drifting hulk." At this grave crisis a Hawaiian appears upon the scene. He was returning to his Island home from the Atlantic seaboard. The captain says of him: "But there was a Sandwich Islander on board, an excellent swimmer, who brought enough liquor and raw pork from below to save our lives." The *Lark* was wrecked on the Island of Kahoolawe. Mr. Hunt bought at the Islands for $10,000 the bark *Peddler,* to go to Astoria, trade with the North instead of the *Lark* and return the Hawaiians to their homes. There is no mention of returning the Hawaiians to their homes (Papers of the Hawaiian Historical Society, No. II, 1904).

the masts and rigging cut away, which caused the vessel to right again, though full of water. One of the hands dived down to the sailmaker's locker, and got out a small sail, which they attached to the bowsprit. He dived a second time, and brought up a box containing a dozen bottles of wine. For thirteen days they had no other sustenance but the flesh of a small shark, which they had the good fortune to take, and which they ate raw, and for drink, a gill of the wine each man *per diem*. At last the trade winds carried them upon the island of *Tahouraka*, where the vessel went to pieces on the reef. The Islanders saved the crew, and seized all the goods which floated on the water. Mr. Hunt was then at *Wahoo*, and learned through some Islanders from *Morotoi*, that some Americans had been wrecked on the isle of *Tahouraka*. He went immediately to take them off, and gave the pilotage of his own vessel to Captain Northrop.

It may be imagined what was the surprise of Mr. Hunt when he saw Astoria under the British flag, and passed into stranger hands. But the misfortune was beyond remedy, and he was obliged to content himself with taking on board all the Americans who were at the establishment, and who had not entered the service of the Company of the Northwest. Messrs. Halsey, Seton, and Farnham[152] were among those who embarked.

When I heard that Mr. Hunt was in the river, and knowing that the overland expedition was to set out early in April, I raised camp at Oak Point, and reached the fort on the 2d of that month. But the brig *Pedlar* had that very day got outside the river, after several fruitless attempts, in one of which she narrowly missed being lost on the bar.

---

[152] After the ruin of the Astoria enterprise, Russell Farnham, one of Astor's men, conferred with Wilson Price Hunt and it was agreed between them that Farnham should undertake to get back to New York by crossing the Pacific ocean and making his way across Siberia and Russia to Europe. This trip around the earth undertook and safely carried out. He took passage on the ship *Pedlar* and crossed over to Siberia. On entering Siberia, Farnham crossed the eastern continent to St. Petersburg, where the American minister to the Russian court presented him to Emperor Alexander as the bold American who had traveled across the empire. The Emperor received him with great kindness and consideration, and sent him on his way to Paris. After great exposure to dangers, toils and sufferings, such a no other man voluntarily submitted himself to for his countrymen, he reached New York, delivered his papers to Astor apprising him of his loss and the ruin at Astoria, and then made his way back to St. Louis (Gaston).

I would gladly have gone in her, had I but arrived a day sooner. I found, however, all things prepared for the departure of the canoes, which was to take place on the 4th. I got ready the few articles I possessed, and in spite of the very advantageous offers of the gentlemen of the N.W. Company, and their reiterated persuasions, aided by the crafty McDougal, to induce me to remain, at least one year more, I persisted in my resolution to leave the country. The journey I was about to undertake was a long one: it would be accompanied with great fatigues and many privations, and even by some dangers; but I was used to privations and fatigues; I had braved dangers of more than one sort; and even had it been otherwise, the ardent desire of revisiting my country, my relatives, and my friends, the hope of finding myself, in a few months, in their midst, would have made me overlook every other consideration.

We quitted Fort George Monday morning, the 4th of April, 1814, in ten canoes, five of which were of bark and five of cedar wood, carrying each seven men as crew, and two passengers, in all ninety persons, and all well armed.

Selected Bibliography

Brackenridge, Henry M., Journal of a Voyage up the Missouri River in 1811 (1814).

Bradbury, John, Travels in the Interior of America in the Years 1809, 1810, 1811 (1986).

Cox, Ross, The Columbia River; Or, Scenes and Adventures During a Residence of Six Years on the Western Side of the Rocky Mountains among various Tribes of Indians hitherto unknown; together with 'A Journey across the American Continent', (1832)

Douglas, Jesse S., ed. "Matthews' Adventures on the Columbia: A Pacific Fur Company Document" Oregon Historical Quarterly 40 (1939), 105-148.

Franchere, Gabriel, Journal of a Voyage on the North West Coast of North America during the Years 1811, 1812, 1813, and 1814, W. Kaye Lamb, ed. (1969).

Henry, A., and Thompson, D., New Light on the Early History of the Greater Northwest, 1799-1814, Henry and Thompson Journals, Vol. II, Elliot Coues, ed. (1897).

Hunt, Wilson P., Nouvelles Annales des Voyages, (1821).

Irving, Washington, Astoria; Or, Anecdotes of an Enterprise Beyond the Rocky Mountains (1836).

Ross, Alexander, The Fur Hunters of the Far
West , Kenneth A. Spaulding, ed. (1956).

------------, Adventures of the First Settlers on the
Oregon or Columbia River, 1810-1813 (1986).

Seton, Alfred, Astorian Adventure: The Journal of
Alfred Seton, 1811-1815, Robert F. Jones, ed.
(1993).

Spaulding, Kenneth A., ed. On the Oregon Trail:
Robert Stuart's Journey of Discovery (1953).

Stuart, Robert, Voyage from the Mouth of the
Columbia to Saint-Louis, on the Mississippi in
1812-13 (1821).

Made in the USA
San Bernardino, CA
11 June 2016